KU-033-544

Introduction

Living Religions is a new R. E. course for the whole primary school, which gives teachers a practical programme of study and clear guidelines for teaching Religious Education. **Living Religions** contains a wide range of flexible classroom activities allowing you to teach, with confidence, the six major world faiths:

 **Christianity**

 **Buddhism**

 **Hinduism**

 **Islam**

 **Judaism**

 **Sikhism**

Who has developed Living Religions?

The series editor is Chris Richards, Inspector for R. E. at the Northamptonshire Inspection and Advisory Service, whose expertise has ensured that the course has been created by a team of experienced R. E. educators and developed in close consultation with members of all respective faith groups. In addition, extensive trialling and consultation with teacher focus groups has ensured the course matches the requirements of all primary teachers.

Course components for Living Religions

Each of the six religions has a Teacher's Resource Book and a supporting Poster Pack. In the case of Christianity, there are two Teacher's Resource Books and two Poster Packs.

Each **Teacher's Resource Book** includes:

- a concise introduction to the religion and key terminology;
- ten units of work based on key themes;
- a wide range of clearly differentiated activities;
- stories for the teacher to read aloud;
- photocopiable activity sheets for independent work.

Each **Poster Pack** includes:

- ten large, A2–size, full–colour posters (one for each unit of work);
- excellent teacher support on the reverse sides, including background information and ideas for discussion.

Living Religions and your Local Agreed Syllabus and the Scottish Guidelines for Religious and Moral Education 5–14

The series has been developed to meet the requirements of the new generation of agreed syllabuses based on the model syllabus guidelines issued by SCAA in 1994.

Living Religions also meets the needs of the first two attainment outcomes in the 5–14 Guidelines relating to Christianity and Other World Religions.

It ensures systematic coverage which gives integrity to the study of each religion. At the same time, a similar series of themes is explored across religions which make it easy to follow a thematic syllabus (see page 1).

Flexibility in the curriculum

Living Religions has been designed to reflect current primary practice by linking with other subjects and allowing for topic-based teaching. It links with other areas of the curriculum not only through content, but also through the development of speaking and listening skills, expansion of vocabulary, inculcation of empathy and understanding, and personal and social skills.

Differentiation in Living Religions

The activities in the Teacher's Resource Books are based on three levels of ability:

- **Core** activities are for children who are broadly of average ability;
- **Extension** activities are for children of higher than average ability or slightly older children;
- **A more basic approach** offers activities suitable for children of lower than average ability or slightly younger children.

Assessment in Living Religions

Many of the activities in **Living Religions** give children a chance to show what they have learned and understood. Their response to these activities can be assessed. The assessment opportunity is shown by the symbol

Additional materials for Christianity

In recognition of the fact that many schools will devote a larger proportion of time to teaching it, two Teacher's Resource Books are provided for Christianity:

Christianity Part 1 Teacher's Resource Book and Poster Pack is suitable for ages 4 to 7;

Christianity Part 2 Teacher's Resource Book and Poster Pack is suitable for ages 7 to 11.

Note: At the end of this Teacher's Resource Book you will find a list of books about Buddhism. We do not recommend these books, but the list includes some books available at the time of writing, should you require extra resources.

Note on terminology: Sanskrit and Pali are in use in the West. In this text Sanskrit has been used.

Buddhism – Some key facts

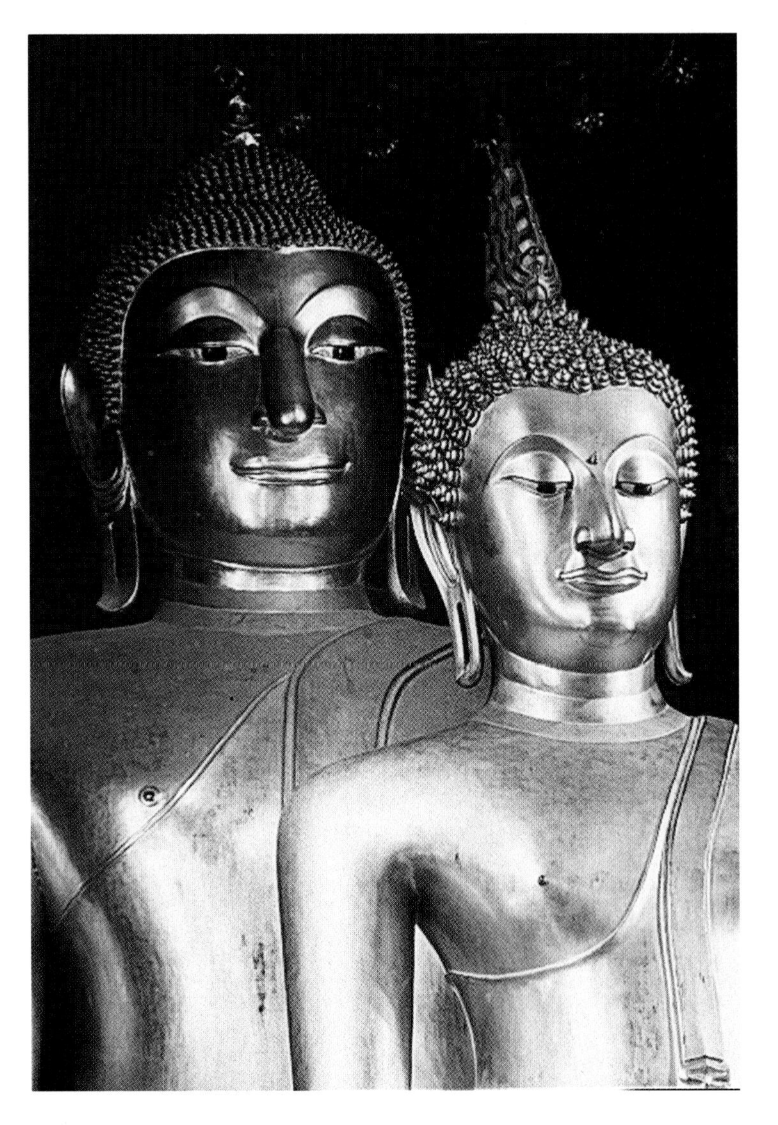

About 500 B. C. in northern India, a prince named Siddhartha Gautama became known to his followers as the Buddha (or 'The Enlightened One'). His insights into the human condition, called 'The Four Noble Truths' and 'The Eightfold Path', are the Dharma (or major teachings) of Buddhism. Buddhists believe that by following these teachings they too may reach the state of enlightenment.

Buddha remains the most important figure in the religion. Images of the Buddha can be found at religious shrines. Buddha is not a God but a symbol of inspiration for Buddhists. When Buddhists go to a shrine or pagoda it is not to worship Buddha, but to show that they are grateful for his teaching.

Teachings about suffering are at the heart of Buddhism. Buddhists strive to be free from suffering and to reach the state of nirvana. Nirvana is the name Buddhists give to a state of complete peace and contentment, of happiness and of freedom from change and suffering. It is not a place but a state of mind and can be achieved before death.

The teachings of Buddhism are written in scriptures, the most important of which is called the 'Tripitaka'. It is quite acceptable for Buddhists not to read scripture, as they believe it is possible to follow the principles of the religion without doing so.

Buddhists believe in karma. This states that all actions and the intentions which lead to actions have a consequence. By following the Eightfold Path, Buddhists aim to make sure that their actions and intentions, and thus the consequences, are positive. Buddhists believe that karma affects one's future life as well as the present life.

Meditation is an important part of Buddhism. There are two types of meditation – one to calm the mind, and one to help people to see the truth about life. Buddhists will meditate on death, Buddha's teachings or an image of Buddha in order to help them to reach a better understanding of truth.

Glossary

Bodhi tree	the tree under which the **Buddha** realised enlightenment
Buddha	the title given to **Siddhartha Gautama** when he found enlightenment. Anyone can become a Buddha. A Buddha is someone who finds enlightenment
Dharma	the teachings of **Buddha**
Dukkha	suffering
Eightfold Path	eight statements that state how to live in order to find true happiness
Enlightened	to have found the truth about life/existence
Five precepts	five rules that a Buddhist will live by in order to live a better life
Meditation	a means of thinking and contemplating
Nirvana	the state of secure, perfect peace in which Buddhists achieve release from being reborn
Sangha	the community of Buddhists
Siddhartha Gautama ***(Gautumma)***	the personal (Siddhartha) and family (Gautama) name of the **Buddha**, the founder of Buddhism
The three universal truths	(1) everything changes; (2) people change; (3) because everything changes, life can never satisfy and makes us suffer
Three jewels	a symbol used to represent the **Buddha**, **Dharma** and the **Sangha** of Buddhism
Tripitaka ***(Trip-ittika)***	the collection of three sections of writings that make up Buddhist teaching
Wesak	the festival day of each month. The festival celebrates the birth, enlightenment and death of **Buddha**

**pronunciations*

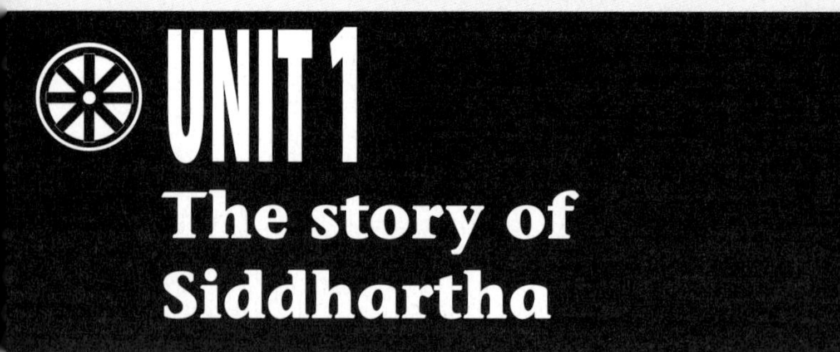

UNIT 1 The story of Siddhartha

AIMS

1 The children should hear the story of the life of Siddhartha Gautama, and be able to recall the main points.

2 The children should encounter the idea of suffering, and recognise that an understanding of suffering is central to the beliefs of Buddhism.

PREPARATION

For these activities you will need:

- poster 1;
- copies of Activity sheet 1 (page 9);
- some small pieces of paper;
- a marker pen for each child;
- glue and scissors.

If possible :

- books and other reference materials on Buddha

You may need to rearrange the classroom furniture for the first activity.

Core activities

1 Exploring feelings
(20 mins)

Sit in a circle/semi-circle to look at the poster. Give each child a marker pen and two pieces of paper. Set the rules:

When you show the poster, the children must look at it and think about how it makes them feel. They should not talk.

Each child should express their thoughts in one or two words and, when asked to, they should write these down on cards.

All the words can then be placed around the poster.

Talk about the different responses. Ask the children to try to group the words that mean something similar.

2 Creating a 'thought poem'
(30 mins)

Either individually or in groups, the children can produce a 'thought poem', which must include the words generated by the class response in Activity 1.

Each child should contribute one line or phrase.

Read/write/display the resulting poems.

3 Class discussion
(10 mins)

Show the children the poster again, and look at it more closely, using the questions and guidance on the reverse of the poster as the basis of a class discussion.

4 About Siddhartha Gautama
(20 mins)

Introduce and then read the story of Buddha (Siddhartha Gautama) on page 10. Use the questions given alongside the story as the basis for a class discussion, to help the children draw meaning from it.

5 Story-making
(40 mins)

Prepare a simple series of pictures which tell the story of Siddhartha Gautama. Give them out of sequence. The children should work out the correct sequence, perhaps as a group, and cut and paste them into the correct order. They can colour the pictures and write the story underneath, or collate the pictures into a storybook.

More able pupils will be able to talk about why Buddha did the things described.

6 Activity sheet 1
(30 mins)

ASSESSMENT OPPORTUNITY

The children should complete Activity sheet 1 (on page 9). Ask them to discuss their answers with someone else doing the same Activity sheet. Ask the children:

Do you agree with each other's answers?

Are there some you disagree about? (Ask them to give reasons why they disagree.)

What do you think the child is feeling?
Why might the child be feeling like this?

EXTENSION THE EIGHTFOLD PATH

Buddha left eight separate steps (The Eightfold Path) to be followed in order to find happiness and enlightenment. Give the children a copy of The Eightfold Path (this is provided on the reverse of the poster). Encourage them to talk about what the steps might mean. Ask the children to draw a path and write the eight instructions on it.

A more basic approach

The suggestions on this page will help you adapt the Core teaching and learning activities, making them suitable for younger children, or those who are at an earlier stage of development.

1 Exploring feelings

Before showing the poster to the children, get them to think about the things that make them happy and those that make them sad.

You can allow each child to draw a picture of one thing that makes them happy and one that makes them sad. Make them into a display. You might then consider adding sad and happy words to the display. (The children can either dictate them or write/copy them with guidance.) These will help them to express themselves when they look at the poster.

2 Writing a 'thought poem'

Use the words you displayed in Activity 1. The children can be encouraged to select five happy and five sad words each. Each word can be used in a sentence which begins: 'I am happy when . . .', or 'I am sad when . . .'. The children should write/copy/dictate their sentences. The sentences can be rearranged to create a poem.

3 Class discussion

The poster can be used in the same way as described in the Core activities, as the children will respond to it according to their level of ability.

4 About Siddhartha Gautama

When telling the story of Siddhartha Gautama, you can use enlarged copies of simple pictures, or overhead transparencies of the pictures to illustrate the story and help keep the children's attention.

5 Story-making

Ask the children to draw pictures to go with the following sentences. You can print out and photocopy the sentences for the children.

Ask them to cut and paste, or copy, the prepared sentences to go with their pictures.

Buddha was a rich prince.

On a journey he saw some sad people. He wanted to help them but he didn't know how.

He sat under a tree and found an answer.

He went and told others his answer.

ACTIVITY SHEET 1

Stepping stones

If you had to give a person eight instructions on how to be happy, what would they be?

1 ________________________

____

2 ________________________

____

3 ________________________

____

4 ________________________

____

5 ________________________

____

6 ________________________

____

7

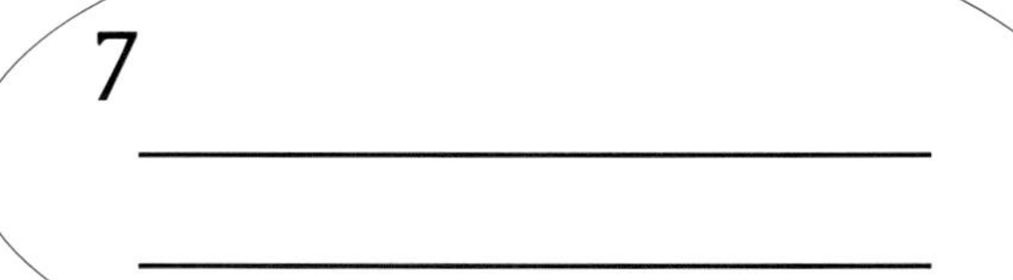

____

____

8 ________________________

____

Introducing the story

There are many stories about the life of Siddhartha Gautama. This story aims to tell of the important events in Buddha's life leading up to, and including, his enlightenment. It does not tell of his later life as 'The Enlightened One'.

The story is set *c.* 563 B. C. E. in Nepal, in the towns of Kapilavastu and Bodh Gaya. It would be useful to look at these on a map with the children so that they are aware of where the story is set.

Talking about the story

The story should be linked to the children's discussion about suffering, in relation to the poster. Ask the children:

- What are the four important things that Siddhartha Gautama saw on his journey? (an old man; sickness; death; a holy man)
- Why did they upset him so much? (because he had not seen anything sad before)
- What do you think Buddha felt when he saw these things? (grief; sadness; sympathy)
- What do you do when you see suffering? (comfort people; give to charity; turn away)
- What did Buddha do to try to find an answer to suffering? (He became a holy man.)
- How did he find an answer? (The answer came to him when he sat under a tree.)
- Where would you go to think about something important? (Encourage the children to identify the 'surroundings' that they would need, e.g. silence, peace, etc.)
- What would you think about?

The story of Siddhartha

Prince Siddhartha had a special chariot that he loved going out in. He liked to see the people of his land lining the streets to smile and wave at him.

But each morning, just as daylight broke (when Prince Siddhartha was still sleeping in his big, soft bed) the King secretly sent his servants out. They went creeping from the palace, so as not to wake Siddhartha.

While the prince was snoring happily, the King's servants rounded up all the sick people in the land; they found all the old and unhappy people and they gathered together all the very poor people. "Stay indoors," they said, pushing them inside their homes. "The prince must not see you, he mustn't know you are here – the King has ordered it!"

One morning, Prince Siddhartha got up very early. He even got up before the servants. The prince called for his special chariot, and he shouted for Channah (his best friend) to come out with him.

At the prince's orders, the King's servant came running, pulling on the reins of the two big, sturdy, white horses which towed the prince's chariot. The servant was very puffed.

"I shan't need you to drive my chariot today," the prince said firmly. "I'm going to drive myself."

The servant was so afraid of what the King would say to him later that all he could do was stutter, "Um. . ." and "but. . .", and then, "Oh, but. . .". Before the servant could finish trying to get his words out, Siddhartha and Channah took the reins and away the chariot rattled, up the palace driveway, leaving him still breathless and wondering whatever would happen next.

Siddhartha drove along roads he had never seen before, where even the stones in the road and the trees along the roadside were unfamiliar to him. The path was dusty and bumpy and there were no happy people smiling at him from below his carriage and waving him along his way.

Suddenly, in the distance, Siddhartha saw the figure of a man. As he rode up closer, he could see that there was something about the man that was very strange. Firstly, the man's body was bent over almost double, and he was walking very slowly, on the thinnest and frailest legs Siddhartha had ever seen. The old man was hauling himself along with the aid of a long and gnarled wooden stick. He could hardly have seen where he was going, because his eyes seemed to be half closed. The man was very ancient, and Siddhartha had never before seen anyone like him.

"What's the matter with that man?" Siddhartha asked Channah, his most trusted friend. "He is very old", Channah replied. "We all get old eventually, even you will." Unlike other people, Siddhartha had never seen anybody so old before. He couldn't quite believe what Channah was saying to him. "Is this what's going to happen to me?" he thought. "And if that's how I'm going to end up, then what's the point?"

On the journey, Siddhartha saw many really terrible sights, which hurt his eyes and made him feel sick and unhappy. He saw many people who didn't have enough to eat, and their clothes were frayed and falling to pieces. These people did not laugh and wave at him. They just stared up at his golden chariot as if they had never seen so much wealth before in their lives. (Some of the people whom Siddhartha saw were so tired and ill, from starvation, that they did not even look up when his carriage passed.)

Then Siddhartha saw a group of men and women emerging from a small hovel by a river. They were shouting instructions to one another. One or two of them were crying, and they were carrying what seemed to be a heavy load on a stretcher - it was a dead body. The men and women tripped and stumbled over rocks and pebbles in their way, as they struggled under the weight of their load.

Next, Siddhartha's chariot passed a holy man wandering along the street with his bowl. Channah explained to Siddhartha that, throughout their land, there were many of these holy men who had chosen to give up their homes and possessions in order to find an answer to their questions. Channah explained that these holy men had no home and had to rely on others to give them shelter and food.

When he finally returned home to his palace, Siddhartha had seen in one day all of the things that the King had kept from him throughout his life. Siddhartha looked around at his home and everything in it seemed different to his eyes. He was very unhappy to live surrounded by beautiful, luxurious things now that he knew that others were suffering. He wanted to be able to help the people he had seen outside the palace gates. But what could he do? Should he give away all of his money?

Siddhartha thought for a long time about what he must do. He thought very hard and very carefully and, finally, he decided that he must leave his life of luxury. He decided that he must go out and become a holy man.

In the middle of the night, Siddhartha prepared his chariot to take him out of the palace and out of the city. Siddhartha then cut off his hair and beard. He took off his prince's clothing and he put on a simple robe. Siddhartha began the life of a holy man.

And Siddhartha lived this life for many years, until he was a very old man himself. His years of thinking about the suffering he saw and felt, of eating very little and sleeping out of doors, had left deep, furrowed lines on his face. But he still didn't know what the answer was.

One day, in despair, Siddhartha sat down underneath a Bodhi tree. He decided not to get up until he had found the answer. He let his thoughts become clear and he relaxed his body so that the answer would be able to come into his mind. Slowly, darkness fell, and Siddhartha sat on, cold and alone, throughout the night. And as the sun started to rise in the morning and the new rays of sunshine started warming Siddhartha's face, he found the answer he was looking for.

Siddhartha got up from under the tree and, from that day onwards, he travelled around telling others about the answer he had found, so that they could also help people. His followers gave him a new name. They called him 'Buddha', which means, 'the one who has found the answer'.

Meditation

AIMS

1. The children should know that meditation is an important part of the Buddhist religion.
2. The children should understand that Buddhists believe that they find out truths about themselves and the world through meditation.
3. The children should have experienced activities which help them to concentrate.
4. The children should have encountered the idea that some decisions are more important than others.
5. The children should have thought about places which are special.

PREPARATION

For these activities you will need:

- poster 2;
- a bell;
- some interesting objects (Activity 2);
- copies of Activity sheet 2 (page 15);
- copies of supplementary activity sheet (page 52).

If possible:

- other books or resources on Buddhism.

Core activities

1 Time to think
(45 mins)

This activity introduces the idea that important things need special times and places for thinking.

Talk with the children about the following questions

- What kinds of important thing might you need to think about?
(An important present to buy; what to spend birthday money on; you've fallen out with your friend – what should you do?)
- If you had to think about something as important as that, where would you do the thinking?
(Encourage the children to identify, e.g. my bedroom, out for a walk, in a special, quiet place.)
- What would help you concentrate?
(Peace, quiet, tidy surroundings/factors individual to all children.)

Ask the children to complete the activity sheet by drawing a background; putting an expression on the face; drawing a body to go with the head; putting words in the thought bubbles. The picture is called: 'Me in a special place thinking important thoughts'.

2 Getting better at thinking
(15 mins)

This activity helps pupils to understand what it is like to meditate. Children can begin to understand what is happening on the poster.

Ask the children to sit in silence and concentrate on an object (e.g. a flower; a coloured vase; a model; a globe) which is visible to them all.

Ask them for how long they are able to concentrate before their mind wanders (usually about four or five seconds).

You can try this a few times, introducing the children to simple rituals to aid their concentration, e.g. sitting straight; eyes closed; with hands flat on a table.

Use a sound, e.g. a clap or a bell, to start and end the period of concentration.

Talk the children through the activity, asking for feedback about their feelings. Do children become aware of getting better? (Emphasize that it is not a competition.) Make sure that the children learn the words 'concentration' and 'meditation'.

Talk about how teachers make sure that pupils are able to concentrate in school, and what children do to help themselves concentrate.

3 Looking at the poster
(30 mins)

Use the questions and guidance on the reverse of the poster as the basis for a class discussion.

Ensure that the practice of Buddhist meditation, as shown on poster 2, is linked firmly to the children's own experience of meditation in Activity 2; talk about similarities and differences.

4 Conclusion
(45 mins)

This activity draws together Activities 1, 2 and 3.

Children should complete the supplementary activity sheet (page 52).

In each column, they should draw pictures or write key words which show how Buddhists meditate, and how they themselves have experienced meditation.

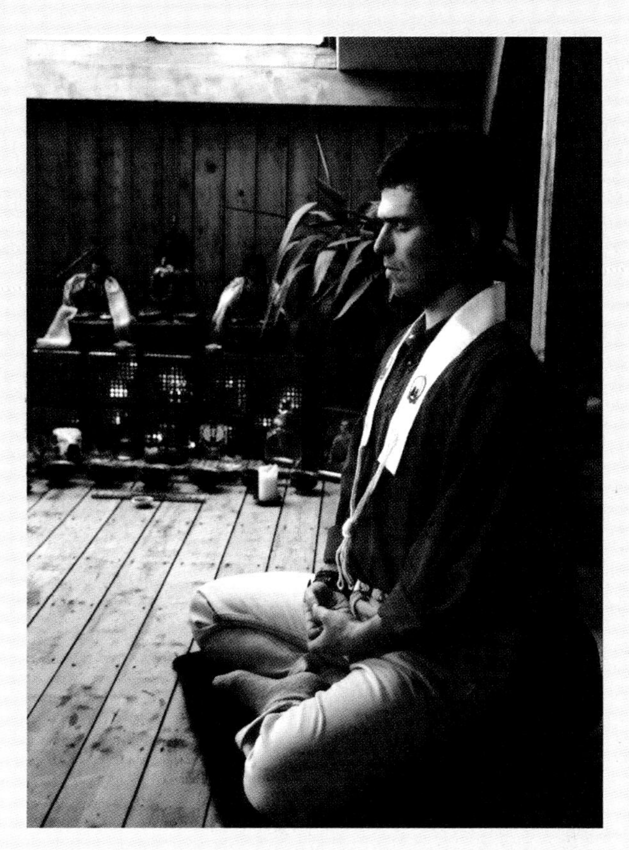

A lay Buddhist meditating

EXTENSION

This activity further develops the idea that symbols can help concentration.

There are many symbols in Buddhism which are used to help concentration when meditating, e.g. the three jewels; the Buddha; the lotus flower.

Find examples and information about some or all of these symbols.

Draw the symbols. Using reference books, label each part with its Buddhist name, and say what each symbolises to a Buddhist.

Some children could explain how these symbols help a Buddhist to concentrate during meditation.

A more basic approach

The suggestions on this page will help you adapt the Core teaching and learning activities, making them suitable for younger pupils or those who are at an earlier stage of development.

1 Time to think

To establish the idea that some things are more important than others, give the children a number of cards with a question written on each, e.g.:

> What should I have for dinner? What shall I do with my £10 birthday money? Who shall I invite to my birthday party? Should I buy a Mars bar or a Bounty? Shall I tell somebody that my friend has stolen something from a shop? What time is it?

You can add a simple picture cue to each card. Go through what each card says, and ask the children to place these questions in order of importance.

Then give the children cards with names and pictures of places, e.g. a football match; my bedroom; the garden shed; a walk on my own; the middle of Woolworths; the bathroom.

Ask them to pick out the best places in which to think about the most important of the questions posed.

Have some blank cards ready if children can add details of their own special place, or an important question to think about.

Use the cards to help children complete Activity sheet 2 (page 15).

2 Getting better at thinking

Expect the children to have only a very short concentration span.

The activity works better if children are in groups with an object on a table in front of them. Use objects which have interesting shapes and colours to hold their attention.

3 Looking at the poster

The discussion is better in small groups. Expect less detail.

Take the pupils through some of the concentration exercises again, to help them to make the link between their experience and the picture.

4 Conclusion

The supplementary activity sheet is not vital for all pupils. Where you do decide to use this with younger/less advanced children, you will need to give the children lots of guidance and allow them to draw some of their answers.

ACTIVITY SHEET 2 Me in a special place thinking important thoughts

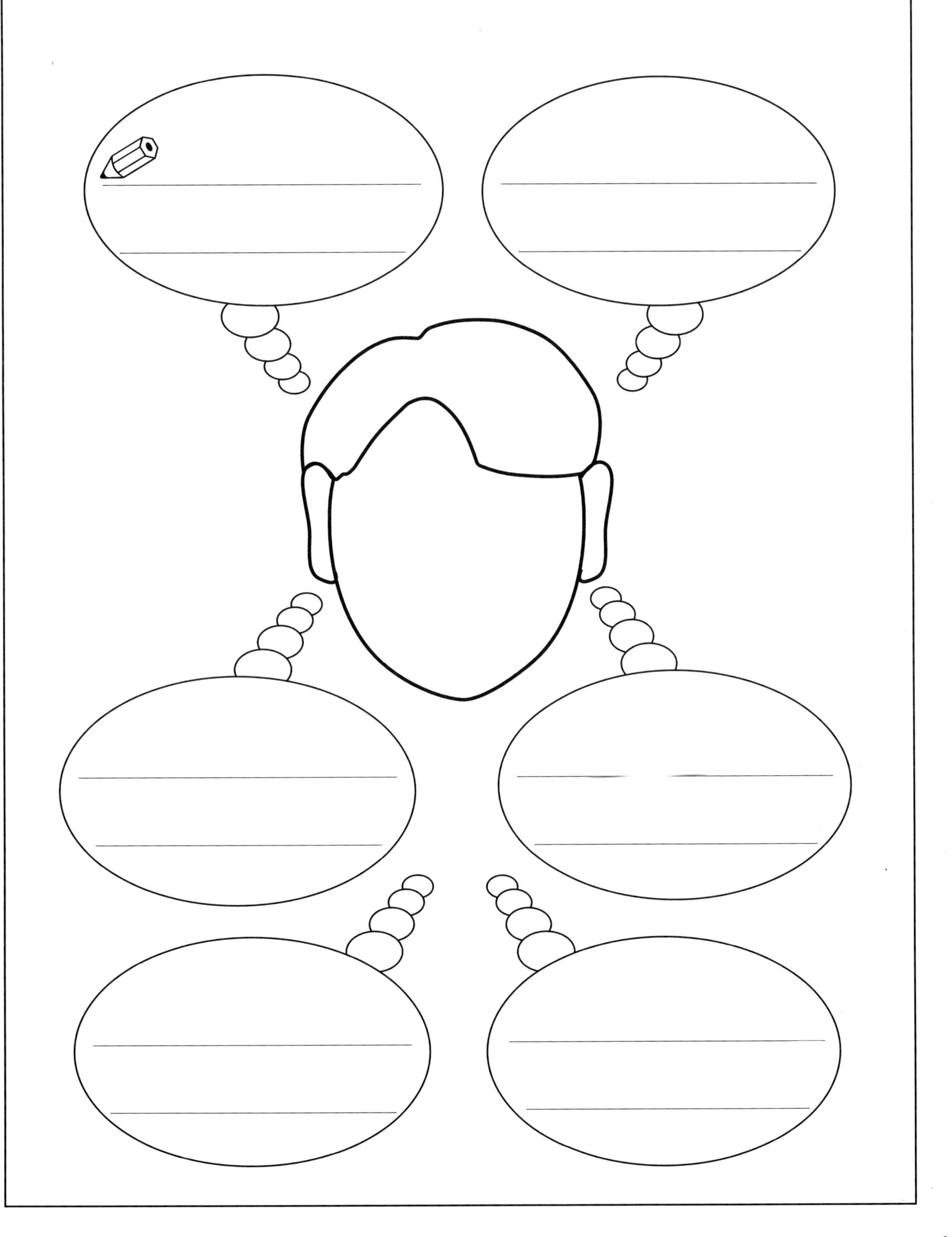

AIMS

1. The children should know what a shrine is.
2. The children should have made decisions about their own important things.
3. The children should have thought about what is important about their school.
4. The children should have been introduced to the special things in a Buddhist shrine.

PREPARATION

For these activities you will need:

- poster 3;
- copies of Activity sheet 3 (page 19) and supplementary activity sheet (page 53);
- objects which celebrate the beliefs and successes of the school (Activity 4).

Core activities

1 Special places: a shrine
(10 mins)

Introduce the children to the word 'shrine'.

Either set the children the task of finding out the meaning of this word, or simply tell them that a shrine is a table, or place, where things that are special or even holy are placed.

2 My special place
(40 mins)

This activity will help the children to think about what is important to them.

Ask them to think about a personal shrine. Talk about the kinds of thing they might want to put in it, the things that they would want to be reminded of.

If necessary, you can use the following imaginary scene to stimulate ideas: you have to move house quickly; which ten things would you choose to take? Encourage the children to look for objects which are special because they are associated with:

special people (friends/family/heroes); special objects; favourite toys; things with special value; things with a special memory attached.

Use Activity sheet 3 (page 19) 'My personal shrine' to record the things which the children choose.

3 Looking at the poster
(40 mins)

This activity extends the children's experience from a personal understanding of the idea of a shrine to an understanding of a shrine in a religious context. Use the questions and guidance on the reverse of the poster in order to help the children to make this link.

Before leaving this activity, try to ensure that all of the children are confident about the meaning of the shrine in a Buddhist context.

4 Making a school shrine
(30 mins)

The first two activities concentrated on things important to individuals. The work on the poster extended this to things important to the Buddhist community.

This activity concentrates on looking at the things that are important to the school community. Talk with the children about your school. Ask

- What does this school stand for? What are its successes? What can it be proud of?
- Where would we find evidence of things important to the school? (code of conduct; school brochure; school badge; trophy display)

Collect evidence and examples, and use the information to make another shrine, perhaps larger than the individual shrines, to celebrate the values and achievements of the school.

The school shrine could be laid out on a table, and incorporate objects (e.g. trophies) or written documents (e.g. behaviour policy).

At a shrine

EXTENSION

You will need the supplementary activity sheet (page 53) for this activity.

The supplementary activity sheet is a word search. The children use what they have learnt to find words to describe the items found at a shrine. They should enter the words in the space below the grid and, if they are able, they should say what each object is used for and explain what it symbolises.

Another place of worship for Buddhists is the pagoda. Ask children to find out information about pagodas, and prepare a booklet or display.

If it is feasible, arrange a visit to a pagoda, a Buddhist temple or monastery, in this country.

Interview the headteacher and/or a governor about what they think is important about the school. Incorporate their responses into the shrine prepared in Activity 4.

A more basic approach

The suggestions on this page will help you adapt the Core teaching and learning activities, making them suitable for younger pupils or those who are at an earlier stage of development.

1 Special places: a shrine

Introduce the word 'shrine' by simply telling the children that a shrine is a table or place where things that are special or even holy are placed.

2 My special place

Use the 'moving house quickly' exercise as a starting point. Activity sheet 3 (page 19) is appropriate for all children, although guidance may need to be given to the children to write/spell the words they choose.

Simplify the task by asking for a response about one thing at a time. Ask leading questions, e.g.

- What is the special object that you would take with you?
- What is your favourite toy?
- What would you take to remind you of special people?
- What is the most expensive thing you would take?
- What do you think your mum/dad/ brother/sister would choose?

In some cases, it might be possible to ask the children to bring in a special object. Help them to write a sentence which says 'This is special to me because. . .'. Write it on a card and place the cards and objects on a display table.

3 Looking at the poster

You can adapt the questions in the following way

- Remember the hard thinking we did? What was it called? (meditation)

Point out the bell and the Buddha.

- Do you remember them? Can you remember what they are for? (to help concentrate; to move on from one stage of meditation to another)

Tell the children that the poster shows a shrine. Reinforce the idea that a shrine is a special place for special things.

Write the names of other important objects shown in the poster on flashcards (table, offerings, special book). Show the flashcards and ask them to identify each object shown in the poster.

The same questions can be asked about these objects as on the poster.

4 Making a school shrine

All children can take part in making the school shrine.

Take the children on a tour of the school, looking for the important things (these will be the same as in the Core activities: code of conduct; school brochure; school badge; trophy display.)

Ask the children to contribute to the shrine by writing with guidance/copying a sentence about the school: "I think this school is important because. . .".

ACTIVITY SHEET 3 My personal shrine

Here is an empty shrine. Fill it with the ten things most important to you. Draw or write them.

Colour and decorate your shrine.

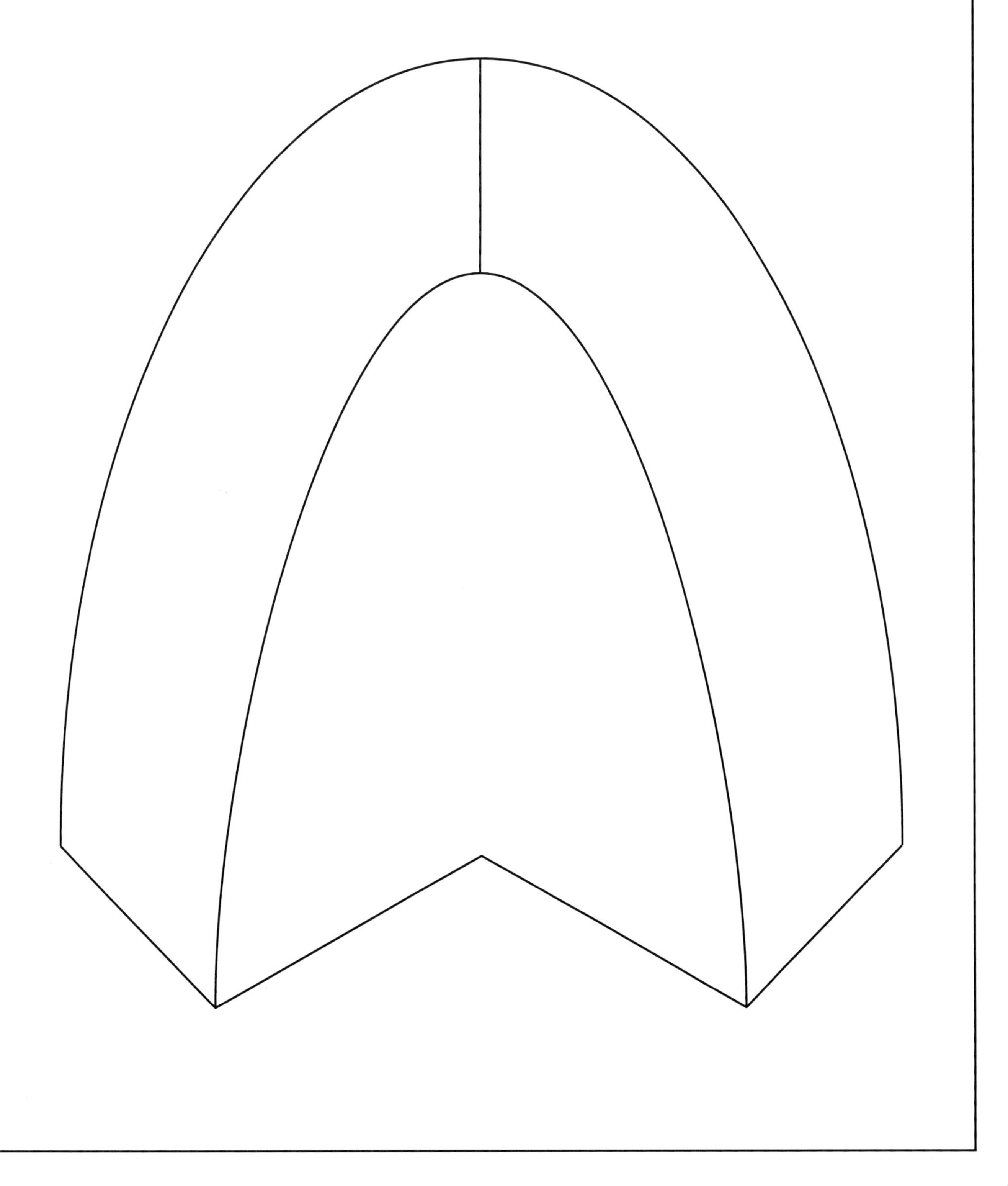

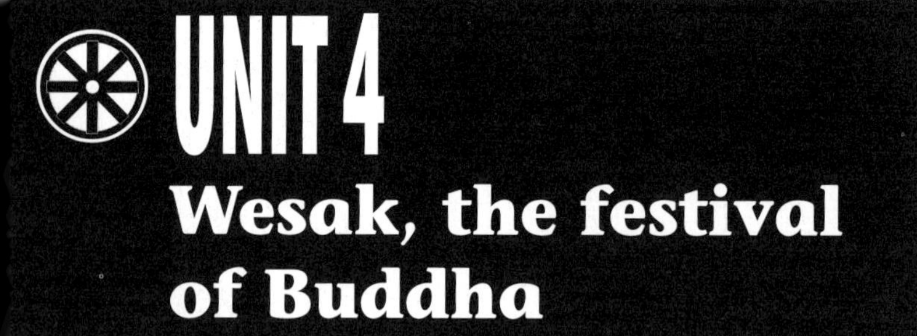

AIMS

1 The children should have developed their understanding of festivals.
2 The children should have become aware that light is a symbol common to festivals in many religions.
3 The children should begin to understand the symbolism of light.
4 The children should know about the festival of Wesak, what it means and how it is celebrated by Buddhists.

PREPARATION

For these activities you will need:

- poster 4;
- Activity sheet 4 (page 23);
- a candle.

If possible:

- reference books on Buddhism (Extension activity);
- word cards ('A more basic approach', Activity 1).

Core activities

1 Celebrating with light
(30 mins)

Children may have done work on festivals before. If so, this can be treated as a revision exercise to remind the children about some of the things they have already discovered about festivals.

With some ceremony and dignified respect, light a candle. Ask the children why they think you have done this. (Look for answers about celebrations and festivals rather than efficiency savings.)

List the events and festivals that the children know about which have light as part of the celebration. Look for answers about Christmas trees; advent candles; birthday candles. If they have done work on any other religions, the children may recall Divali in Sikhism and Hanukkah in Judaism. (Encourage the children to identify that these festivals are often anniversaries.)

Focus on birthdays. Use Activity sheet 4 (page 23) to record the ways in which birthdays are celebrated. Children can write short sentences and illustrate the activity sheet.

Ask the children

- Why do we celebrate birthdays? (Encourage the children to develop their answers from simply 'Birthdays celebrate the day you were born', to identifying that a birthday marks another milestone in the journey through life.)

Many of the children will have mentioned, or written/drawn on their activity sheet, candles on a birthday cake. Return to the candle you lit earlier, and remind the children of the observation that light is often used in festivals. Ask the children why they think this might be. (Look for answers about symbols, light representing life, or goodness.)

2 Looking at the poster
(30 mins)

Use the questions and guidance on the reverse of the poster for this activity.

Ensure that you make the link between the candles used in the Buddhist celebration of Wesak and light in other celebrations.

Encourage the children to pick out any other similarities between the festival of Wesak and other celebrations they know e.g. giving cards; making offerings and giving gifts; going to places of worship.

3 Take me to your party
(60 mins)

Through Activities 1 and 2, the children should have developed a better understanding of celebrations and festivals, and a wider vocabulary with which to describe celebrations and festivals.

This activity asks children to apply their learning through an imaginative story. Set the following scene and the task:
Write a story based on the following events.

> You are at home. You are having a birthday party. (The party could be yours, or for another person in the family.)
>
> There is a knock on the door.
>
> You answer it, and find an alien standing there.
>
> Invite the alien in.
>
> The alien is very curious about the party.
>
> Explain to the alien what is happening, and why.

Use Activity sheet 4 (page 23) to help you.

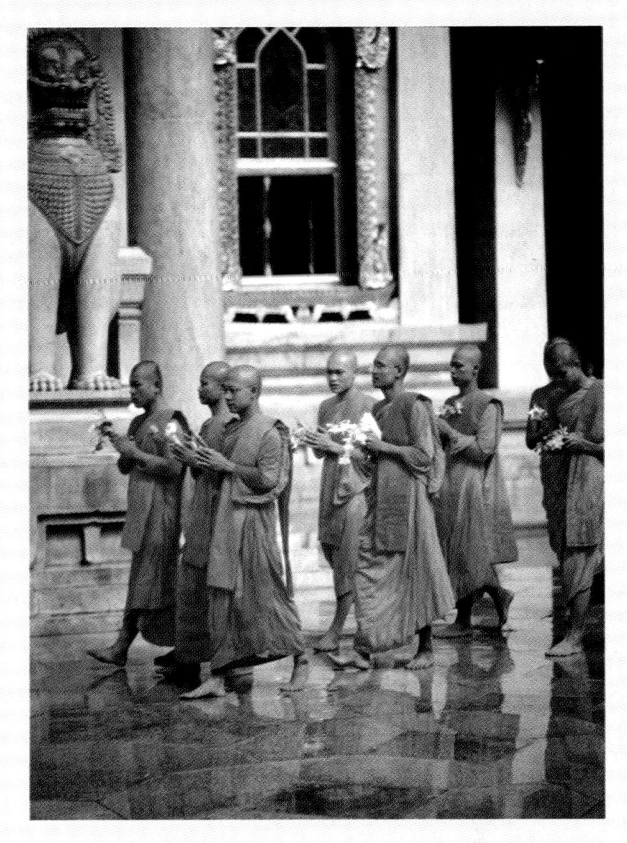

Monks with flowers, incense and candles

EXTENSION

The festival of Wesak celebrates the birth, enlightenment and death of the Buddha. The story of the Buddha's enlightenment is told on pages 10 and 11, but there is little detail about his birth or death.

Children can find out more about these events in the life of the Buddha using other resources. The following books are helpful references: *Stories from the Buddhist world*, published by Macdonald; *Leaders of religion – Buddha*, published by Oliver and Boyd.

The children can use their research to help them to create a piece of drama, a storyboard, or a children's book. They can tell the story to the class.

Ensure that the children are clear about the important and special events in the life of Buddha. They should look at the stories in some detail and consider their answers.

A more basic approach

The suggestions on this page will help you adapt the Core teaching and learning activities, making them suitable for younger pupils or those at an earlier stage of development.

1 Celebrating with light

The first part of the Core activity – lighting the candle – is a suitable introduction to this activity for all children.

When you come to use Activity sheet 4 (page 23) you can, where necessary, generate a set of sentences/words for the children, which can be copied or cut out and pasted onto the activity sheet.

In order firmly to establish the idea that we can celebrate our growth and change with age, prepare a few very simple pictures to illustrate what children learn to do at different ages, e.g. learning to: walk; ride a bike; read; swim; talk; write etc.

Ask the children to put these into a likely chronological order, and make the point that both growth and new achievements are worth celebrating.

To establish ideas about light as a symbol in celebrations, you can make some cards marked with the following words: life; death; good; bad; beginning; ending; pure; dirty.

Ask the children to pick out those which they feel to be associated with the lighted candle, and place the words around it.

2 Looking at the poster

The questions and guidance on the reverse of the poster are suitable for all children.

Discussions in small groups will help to ensure that all children have a chance to contribute and participate.

3 Take me to your party

You can set the scene for the story as in the Core activities.

The story–writing will need much more guidance.

Talk to the children about what would be said, and, if necessary, write the words for them to copy or stick onto the page.

Place them in order down the left-hand side of an A4 page.

The space on the right-hand side is for writing about what you would tell the alien.

Ask the children to draw pictures of the five things you might find at a birthday party. They can write sentences to explain what is happening in each picture.

ACTIVITY SHEET 4

On my birthday

On my birthday this is what happens. . .

1 Draw . . .	
2 Draw . . .	
3 Draw . . .	

Here are some words to help:

cake candles cards presents friends party family special.

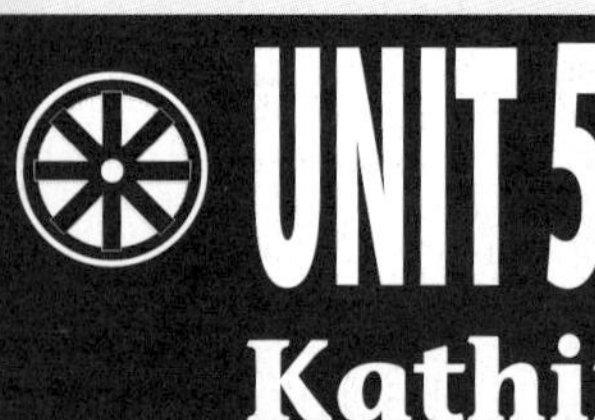

UNIT 5 Kathina Day, celebrating monasteries

AIMS

1 The children should know what happens on Kathina Day.

2 The children should understand the relationship between monks and lay people.

3 The children should be introduced to the idea of 'making merit'.

PREPARATION

For these activities you will need:

- poster 5;
- board games made using Activity sheet 5 (page 27) and supplementary activity sheet (page 54);
- counters and dice for playing the games;
- 'moral dilemmas' (Extension);
- a carrier bag and packages ('A more basic approach', Activity 1).

Core activities

1 A difficult journey (30 mins)

Arrange the children into groups of between four and six.

Give each group a card with the following description

You are a group of monks.

As a group, you are about to go on a long journey together, which will take several months.

You will walk along dusty roads and rocky paths and through forests. It will take you several days to travel between each town or village.

You each have:

1 good sandals and a thick robe;

2 one strong bag the size of a supermarket carrier bag;

3 a wooden bowl;

4 a very small amount of money;

5 a water bottle.

To survive, you will need to rely on the generosity of the people you meet.

Decide as a group:

- What shall we take in each bag?
- What can we do for people so that they will give us food and shelter on our journey?
  (Describe helping them in words and actions.)
- What are ten good words to describe the journey?
  (Encourage the children to describe: people you meet and their generosity, or otherwise; the scenery; the hardships of travel/obstacles to overcome.)

2 Looking at the poster
(30 mins)

This activity is designed to help children to understand what it is like to be a Buddhist monk on his journey.

You can introduce the poster by explicitly making this link, explaining to the children that they have planned some journeys using their imagination, but some people actually go on this kind of journey.

Show the children the poster and use the questions and guidance on the reverse of the poster as the basis for a class discussion.

Before leaving this activity, try to ensure that the children:

1 know about Kathina Day;

2 relate to the feelings of the people involved.

3 The travel game
(60 mins)

Playing the board game (Activity sheet 5, page 27 and supplementary activity sheet, page 54) will help the children firmly to establish the knowledge about Buddhism and Kathina Day which they have gained so far.

Activity sheet 5 (page 27) gives a blank board for the game. The text for the cards is on the supplementary activity sheet (page 54).

The children can colour and decorate the boards with suitable Buddhist symbols. Cards should be placed face down on the board.

Divide the class into groups. Players in each group should throw the dice in turn, and move along the monks' road. The player who reaches the end first wins.

If they land on a coloured square, the children should take a card and follow the instructions.

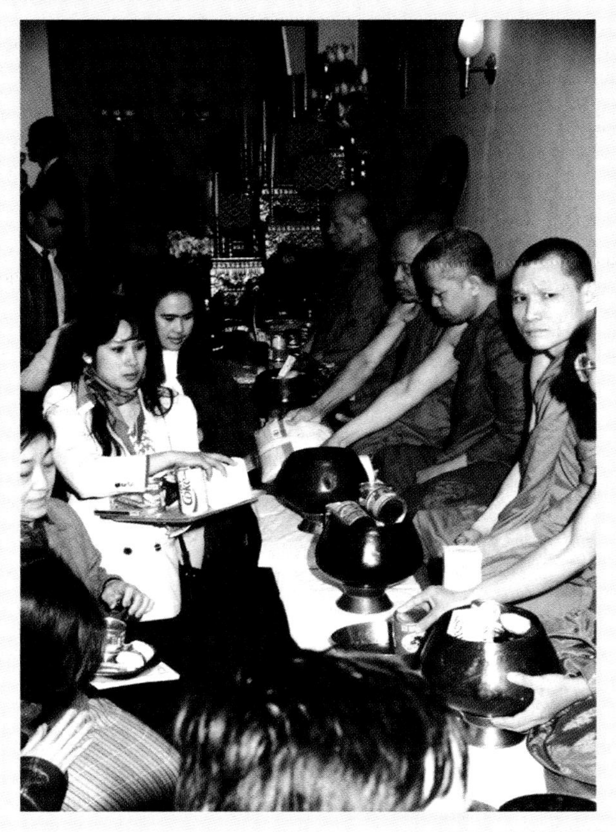

Lay Buddhists giving to monks on Kathina Day

EXTENSION

This activity extends the idea of 'making merit', first introduced on the reverse of poster 5.

Set the children one or more moral dilemmas, e.g. you see your friend taking sweets from another child's bag; you find a £10 note in the classroom; you know you can persuade Mum to take you to the cinema, but you know she can't really afford it; you find a purse with some money and a name and address inside.

For each situation, ask the children to write about or describe: the right thing to do; the wrong thing to do; what might happen if I do the right thing; what might happen if I do the wrong thing.

There are many possible answers and consequences. The object of this exercise is for children to recognise: the different possibilities; that some replies are more 'moral' than others; that rewards are not always tangible; and that feeling good about what you have done is important.

A more basic approach

The suggestions on this page will help you adapt the Core teaching and learning activities, making them suitable for younger children or those at an earlier stage of development.

1 A difficult journey

The children will need more help to understand the situation and the task. Talk to them about the journey, simplify the card, and only use it as a reminder.

To help the children learn from having to decide what to take, you can make this a practical activity. Give each group one carrier bag and a number of different-sized packages, some oddly shaped, which do not all fit into the bag at the same time.

Label the packages: extra food; a tool kit; soap and toothpaste; books to read; a pillow; sweets; my teddy; a sewing kit; fishing line and hooks; a ball of string; spare clothes; a food bowl; knife; fork; spoon; a cup.

Ask the children to choose enough items to fill their bags. They should tell you why they have chosen some things and left others behind.

Talk with the children about how difficult such a journey would be.

2 Looking at the poster

The poster introduces the idea of making merit. This is a concept which can be broadly understood by all children. You can build on this idea by giving the children moral dilemmas to consider. Give the children simple dilemmas and offer them only two alternatives, e.g.

> I find a purse. Alternatives: I keep the purse or I give the purse to the police.
>
> I see my friend taking sweets from somebody's bag. Alternatives: I say nothing to anybody or I tell the friend to put the sweets back.

Ask the children to describe how they would feel in each case. Encourage them to talk about their feelings towards the other people involved (the purse's owner; their friend etc.).

The children can draw simple expressions on face shapes to show their feelings.

Encourage the children to recognise that some alternatives are 'better' than others.

3 The travel game

All children can play the game.

The main difficulty will be in reading the cards, so the teacher/adult/assistant, or another child, will need to help with the reading.

ACTIVITY SHEET 5 The travel game

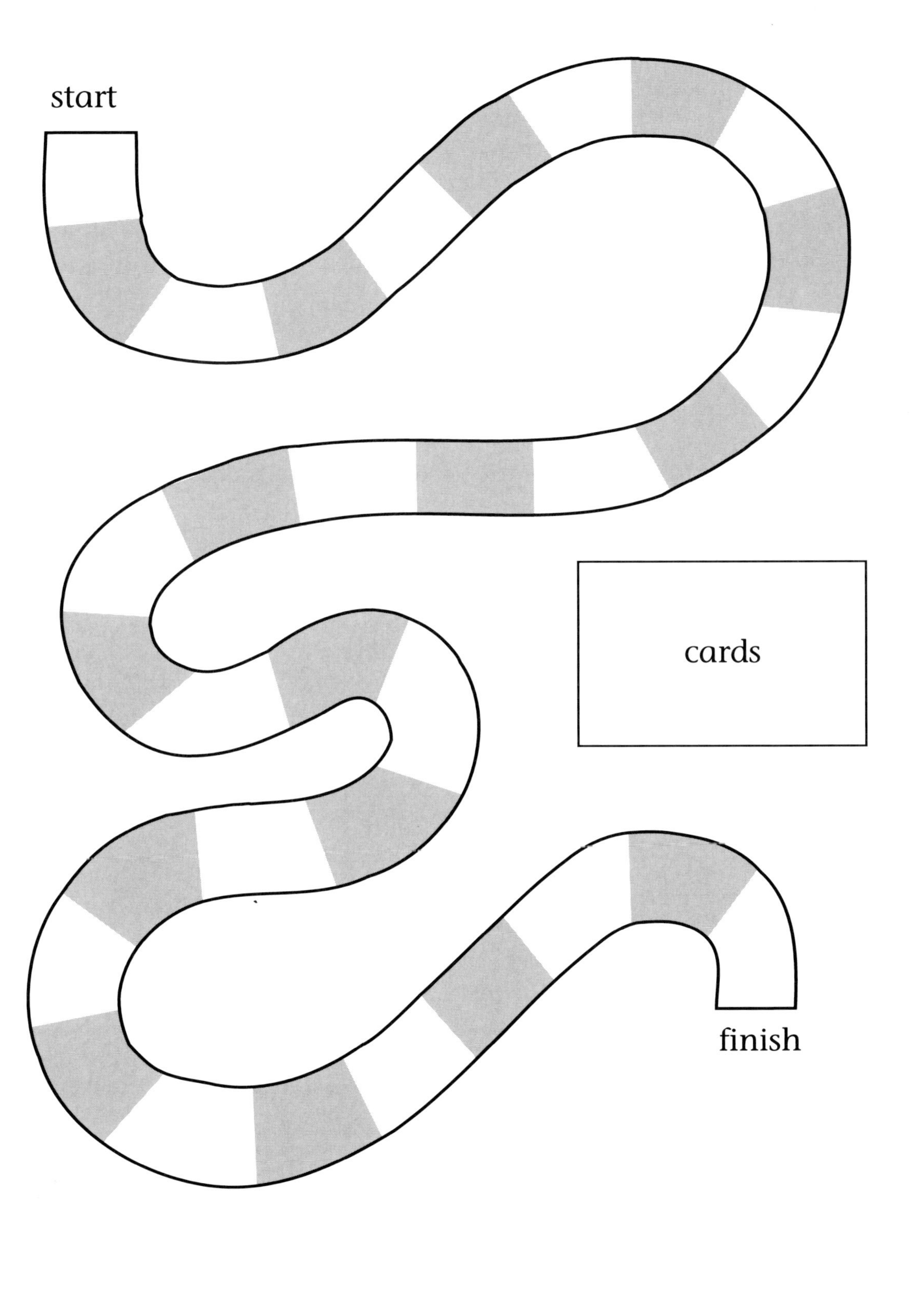

UNIT 6 The Tripitaka, the holy book of Buddhists

AIMS

1 The children should know the name of the Buddhist scriptures.

2 The children should be able to recognise that the scriptures are important to Buddhists.

3 The children should have heard a story from the Buddhist scriptures.

PREPARATION

For these activities you will need:

- poster 6;
- examples of slogans or jingles from the television;
- mask shapes (Activity sheet 6, page 31);
- elastic and materials for making masks (Activity sheet 6).

Core activities

1 Introduction
(20 mins)

If the children have encountered the following discussion already, it will still be useful for them to revise and recount the ideas they expressed.

Explain to the children that some books are special because they are about people's religious beliefs. Ask them to name some special books (some of those named will be religious, some not). Ask the children

- What makes these books special? (wisdom; knowledge and information; holiness; links with Gods/religion)

Tell the children that it is not difficult to learn things by heart. Find some common slogans, jingles or catch phrases from the television. Give the children the first two or three words and ask them to complete the sentence, e.g. say 'neighbours' and expect the reply 'everybody needs good neighbours'.

After you have been through a few similar examples with the children, ask them why they are so clever at remembering these. Encourage the children to identify some of the following answers: they have heard them so many times; the words have a good rhythm and rhyme; because they are interesting and important. Ask the children to remember this activity, because they will need to talk about it again in the next activity.

2 Looking at the poster
(30 mins)

Use the questions and guidance on the reverse of the poster as the basis of a class discussion.

Ensure that the children are introduced to the important facts about the Tripitaka.

3 The story of the monkeys and the hunter
(30 mins)

Read the children the story on page 32. Use the questions given as the basis of a class discussion, to draw meaning from the story.

As well as learning more about the beliefs of Buddhism, the children should know that this is an example of a story taken from the Sutra Pitaka, one of the holy books of Buddhists.

4 A play
(40 mins)

Activity sheet 6 (page 31) shows how the children can make masks for characters in the story. The characters are: the two monkey brothers; the monkey mother; the cruel hunter; the wise teachers; the hunter's wife and children.

Use a photocopier to enlarge the faces to the correct size. Give each character either a monkey face or a human face. Ask the children to decorate the face to show its character.

Divide the story into scenes. Allocate a group of children to each scene. Each group has to make masks and play the characters. You can act as a narrator, telling the story. The children can then act out the scenes. (You may wish to give them 'speech' cards, showing what they should say when the narrator cues them to speak.)

Talk to the children about each of the characters in the story and what their feelings would be in that situation and in each scene.

You may decide to allow the children to get into smaller groups, allocating the different roles to each other and playing out the story to show to the rest of the class later.

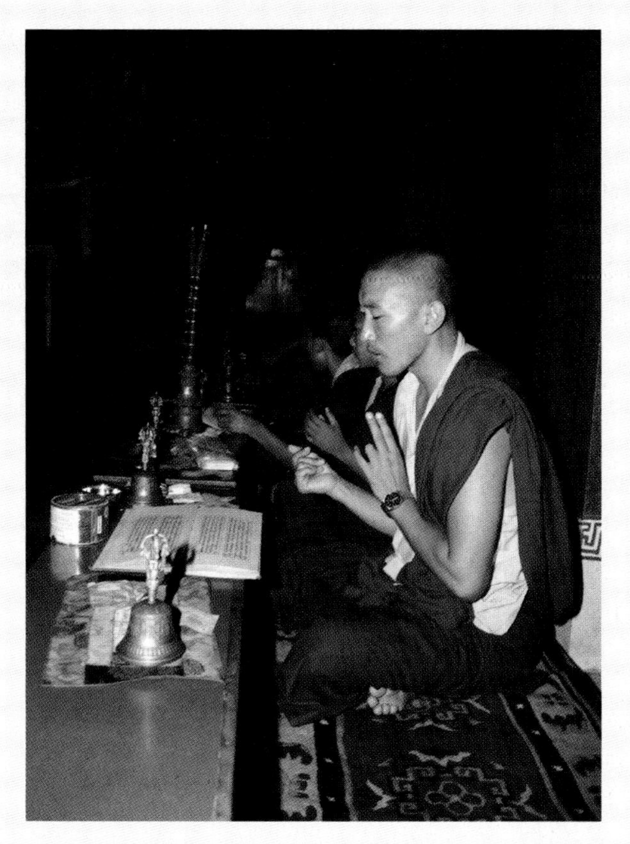

Buddhist holy book

EXTENSION

Find an illustration of the Buddhist wheel of life, and a description of the idea of reincarnation: the wheel should show several situations in life, many of which are unpleasant. Buddhists believe that the soul of a person continues to be reborn into new lives, the quality of which depend on actions in the previous life.

The aim of the Buddhist is to break free from this wheel, and not suffer within it in any form. Whilst they continue to be reborn, they are trapped within the wheel, with the cycle of life going on and on. They believe that when they are enlightened they can break free from being reborn. They call this state nirvana.

Ask the children to draw the wheel, and describe the idea of rebirth. Talk with them about these questions:

Why do Buddhists use the wheel as a symbol of rebirth?

What do you think of the idea of rebirth?

A more basic approach

The suggestions on this page will help you adapt the Core teaching and learning activities, making them suitable for younger pupils or those at an earlier stage of development.

1 Introduction

The Core activity is suitable for all children, but you can make the activity more practical and visual by:

1 Showing the children some special books, e.g. Bibles; school log book; record book.

2 Videoing some advertisements with catchy jingles. Play the first line, and see whether children can carry on.

2 Looking at the poster

The guidance for discussion based on the reverse of the poster is suitable for all children. You can explain about the Tripitaka and reinforce the children's understanding of the holy book in the following ways

Draw the outline of a book.

Show the children three baskets or small boxes.

Place cards in the shape of a leaf in each. Explain to the children that a very long time ago, the special book of Buddhists would have been written on leaves.

Write the words: 'rules', 'teaching', 'higher teachings' on each leaf.

The children will be able to understand at a simple level the relationship between the three baskets (with different kinds of important writing in them) and the book which is special to Buddhists.

3 The story of the monkeys and the hunter

The story is appropriate for all children.

The questions given with the story are suitable for all children, and can be differentiated by response.

Tell the story in episodes, and talk about one episode at a time.

4 A play

The children will need some help with their masks. You can talk to them about how to show character on masks. (Give some examples for the children to copy.)

For the play based on the story, help the children to prepare very simple role–plays of different scenes from the story.

Alternatively, read the script and ask children to mime the actions.

ACTIVITY SHEET 6 Making masks

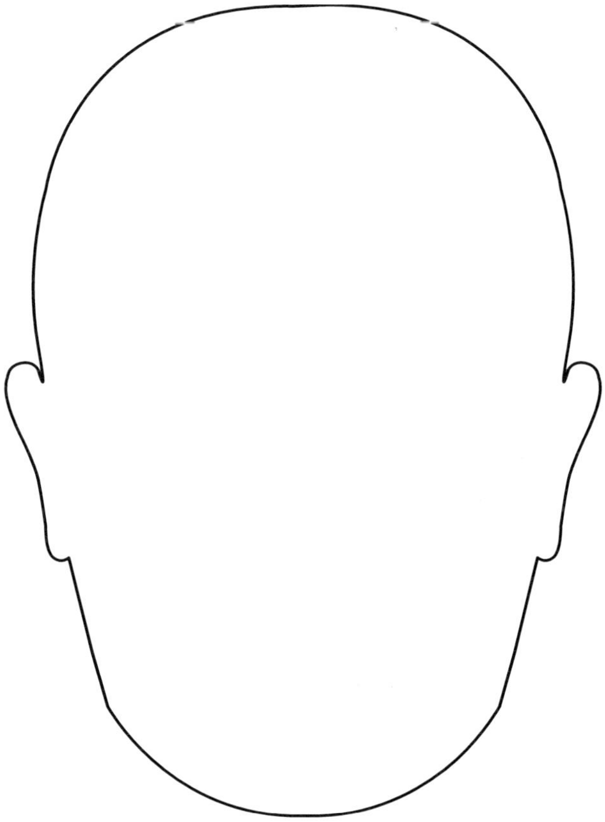

Introducing the story

Explain to the children that Buddhists believe in other lives after this one, and that the things people do in this life will have a bearing on what happens to them in the next life. Therefore, it is important to gain merit or make merit in life. (See the reverse of poster 4 for more information on making merit.) Try to be wary of becoming too deeply involved in teaching the children about rebirth.

Ensure that the children know that the story of the monkeys and the hunter is an adaptation of a story from the Tripitaka, and is about the Buddha in a past life, when he was a monkey. The story can be used to introduce or reinforce the idea that not all stories in holy books are meant to be taken literally. Clearly this is a story with a message, rather than a simple description of events.

Without placing too much emphasis on particular examples, note that not all the stories in other holy books are meant to be taken literally. It is important that the children understand that this doesn't mean that the story is a lie, but rather that the writer hid his meaning in the story for us to dig out, or told the story to make a point more clearly.

Talking about the story

When talking about the story, encourage the children to think particularly about:

1 descriptions of the characters;

2 what the consequences of their actions might have been.

- Who was the bravest in the story?
  (Monkeys.)
- What happened in the story which shows you how much the monkeys loved their mother?
  (They died for her.)
- Why was the hunter so upset at the end of the story?
  (He realised what a nasty person he was.)
- What do you think he should have done next?
  (Encourage the children to suggest that he might have tried to make up for his wrongdoings.)
- What do you think the story is trying to teach Buddhists?
  (You need to be good in life; not all rewards are immediate.)
- Is it always the case that bad behaviour results in bad things happening and good results from good?
  (If the children give a negative answer, you can give examples of where this is not the case, suggesting also that even where bad behaviour may appear to have paid off, there will have been some other personal cost, e.g. feelings of guilt; the individual becoming unpopular etc. Similarly, where good behaviour appears not to have been rewarded there may be some good consequence in the future. Make the point to the children that Buddhists believe that it is worth doing good for its own sake.)
- Was the action of the two brothers good?
- If so, is it good that they died?

The story of the monkeys and the hunter

In a city, high in the mountains and close by the forest, there once lived a horrible young man. He was always yelling and fighting, and threatening to beat people up. Although he was clever, even his teachers shuddered when they had to be near him. But at last he was finished with learning and ready to go out into the world, so that they all breathed a great sigh of relief.

"Just you watch out!" the teachers warned him when he said goodbye. "If you don't get rid of that nasty streak of yours you'll regret it one day."

But the young man just laughed. Then he set out to seek his fortune. He travelled about here and there; and all the time he was trying to find some steady work, something that would make him rich. But he never managed to keep any job for very long, because he was always bullying the other workers and criticising the boss. He tried this and he tried that, without any real success. In the end, having married and had some children along the way, he decided it would be best to work for himself.
So he set himself up as a hunter.

Of course, hunting was not the sort of work that would ever make him rich but, nevertheless, it suited him very well. He took great pleasure in creeping up on the unsuspecting wild animals, seeing their red blood spurt out as his arrow hit them, and hearing their screams. He really enjoyed tearing the beautiful fur from their broken bodies to sell in the market, and chopping up their flesh for meat.

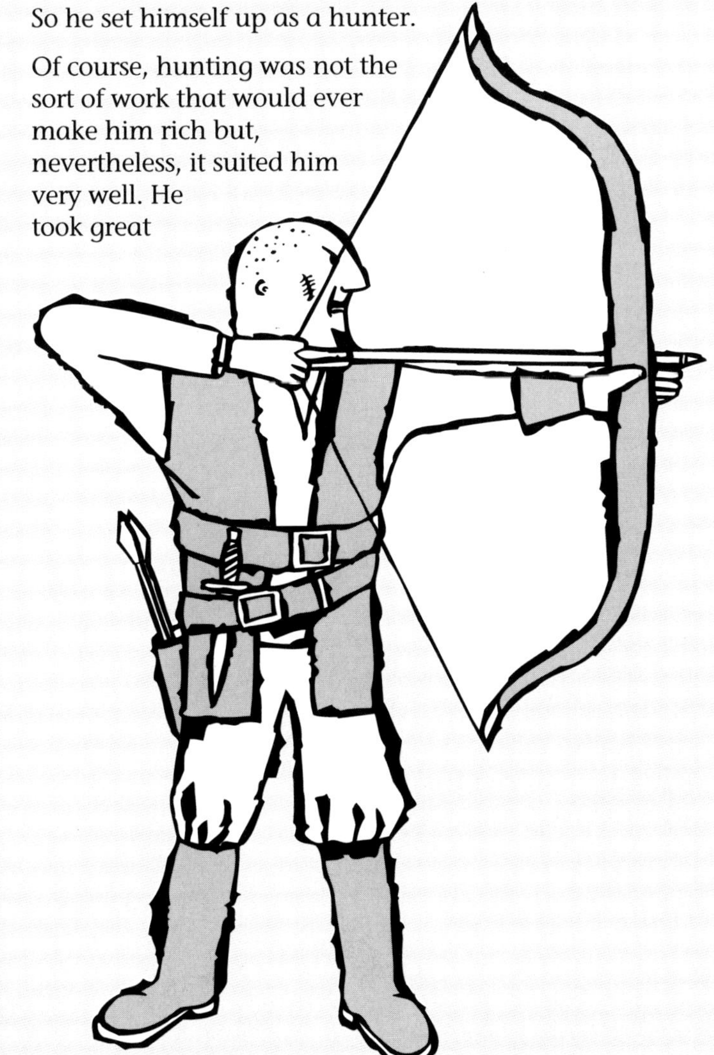

One day, as he was stalking through the forest, he suddenly saw three monkeys. Two were young males, and they were making a great fuss, chattering at and grooming the third one, who was their old, blind mother. The hunter raised his bow to shoot them, but at that moment the young ones looked up and saw him.

They understood perfectly what he was going to do.

"Stop!" screeched the older monkey brother. But the hunter just spat at the ground and hurried to take aim.

"Please, please, please!" screeched the monkey, "don't shoot my poor, dear, old mother! And I beg you to spare the life of my little brother too. If you really have to kill any of us, just go for me!"

The hunter answered with a cruel laugh. He shot the elder monkey brother dead. Then he took aim again.

"No!" screamed the younger monkey brother. "Don't kill my beloved mother. If you really, really won't stop, please, please shoot me instead of her!"

So, still laughing, the hunter shot him. Now the whole forest seemed to be shocked into silence. The old monkey mother sat very still, trembling as she hid her blind eyes in her paws. The hunter took aim for the third time and killed her too.

Then he tied the dead monkeys together into a pathetic bundle, slung them over his shoulder and, whistling cheerfully to himself, set off for home.

Well, he was almost there when a powerful storm blew up. Thunder rumbled and rain pelted down. The hunter began to run – but just as he came out of the trees, a great bolt of lightning suddenly flashed out of the sky – and he saw it strike his little house and turn it into a blazing fireball!

Now the hunter screamed, just as the monkeys had done – but, just as for them, it was no use. In a cloud of black smoke, the house collapsed into a heap of charred ruins.

As he stood there, staring at it in horror, for the first time he saw what a dreadful, cruel life he had made for himself. But it was too late now to change the terrible things he had done in the past. Struck with horror at the thought of his own wickedness, he sank down among the ruins of his home.

There beside him lay the sad bodies of the three dead monkeys: the good old mother and her two brave, kind sons. Each of them had cared more for each other than for itself; each, in its own way, had lived a good life.

The Sangha, the family of Buddhism

AIMS

1 The children should know that all Buddhists belong to the Sangha.

2 The children should know that this is the collective name for Buddhists.

3 The children should have encountered the concept of interdependence.

4 The children should have reflected on the experience of belonging and not belonging.

PREPARATION

For these activities you will need:

- poster 7;
- copies of Activity sheet 7 (page 37);
- cards, pictures, objects ('A more basic approach').

If possible:

- some artefacts which denote membership of a group, e.g. uniforms, badges.

Core activities

1 Belonging
(30 mins)

This activity is designed to highlight the ways in which people belong to different groups, and are interdependent on each other.

Brainstorm the different groups to which children in the class belong. Look for:

1 organisations such as Cubs, Brownies;

2 teams and/or sporting/recreational groups;

3 family groups;

4 friendship groups;

5 the school community;

6 any other.

- How do you show membership of a group?
  (uniforms; taking a special name; abiding by a common set of rules; participating in group activities)
- What do people in groups do for each other?
  (Encourage the children to identify: help; support; enable people to do what they want; give a sense of importance.)

Make a display to show the various groups to which the children belong. Use the artefacts and evidence that children contribute, either from the groups to which they belong or from research they have done.

2 Not belonging
(30 mins)

Activity 1 looks at the benefits of belonging; this activity looks at the experience and feeling of not belonging.

Read the children the story on page 38. Use the questions and guidance given as the basis of a class discussion.

3 Looking at the poster
(30 mins)

Use the questions and guidance on the reverse of the poster as the basis of a class discussion.

Ensure that:

1 the idea of interdependence is reinforced and discussed;

2 you draw on children's experiences of belonging and not belonging to allow them better to understand the benefits Buddhists have from belonging to the Sangha.

4 Interdependence
(30 mins)

This activity will help the children firmly to establish the idea in their minds that Buddhist monks and lay people have responsibilities to each other.

Activity sheet 7 (page 37) shows drawings of Buddhist monks/nuns and lay people. Below are a number of statements which describe what it is like to be part of the Sangha, and what responsibilities different people have.

1 I spend a lot of time meditating.

2 I collect food in my bowl.

3 I teach other people about the Buddha.

4 I lead ceremonies and worship.

5 I visit the monastery and give food to monks.

6 I learn about the Buddha from monks.

7 The monks help me run important ceremonies.

8 I am different from everybody else, but we are all equal.

The children can match the statements to the relevant picture. They can do this by writing the number of the sentence in the right speech bubble. The first one has been given for them.

Belonging to the Sangha

EXTENSION

Build on and develop the children's investigation into the different groups to which people belong. Set the pupils the following task

1 Make up some simple questions to find out to which groups, clubs or organisations other children in the school belong.

2 Collect this information from as many people as possible.

3 Organise your findings into a chart or picture which shows the number of different groups or organisations, and the number of children in each group.

A more basic approach

The suggestions on this page will help you adapt the Core teaching and learning activities, making them suitable for younger pupils or those at an earlier stage of development.

1 Belonging

Make cards with the names of different groups. Ask the children to identify or select those that they belong to. Groups could include: my family; this school; this class; the football team; Cubs/Brownies etc.; the fire brigade; the recorder club; swimming club. Use your knowledge of the children to create the cards.

Include some blanks, so that you can add new groups in discussion with the children.

Talk about how they show that they belong, and what the members of these groups do for each other. Find and talk about artefacts which identify group membership. Ask the children to bring these in, if possible.

2 Not belonging

The story and questions given are appropriate for all ages and abilities. When the children come to consider who they rely on, give them pictures of people who help, e.g. police; mothers; crossing attendants. Talk with them about the ways in which these people help. Write the words which the children use around the pictures.

To help children think about what it would be like if that person didn't exist, give them the start of a sentence, e.g. 'If there were no policemen. . .'

Ask the children to write with guidance/ copy an end to the sentence, or simply respond verbally, in discussion.

3 Looking at the poster

Prepare large pictures of the objects which a monk would have. Ask the children to match the large picture to the object on the poster that relates to it, e.g. picture of razor to shaved head etc. If possible, collect examples of the objects a Buddhist monk would have. Let children handle them and talk about them (use a very blunt darning needle, and an imitation razor!).

4 Interdependence

The children may need help with reading the statements on Activity sheet 7 (page 37), and should be encouraged and guided to put the right statement against the correct picture.

Focus on the Buddhists' feelings of belonging to their group, and the fact that they have different roles in helping each other.

ACTIVITY SHEET 7

Buddhist monks

Look at the sentences below. Write the number in the right speech bubble. Talk about your answers.

1 I spend a lot of time meditating.

2 I collect food in my bowl.

3 I teach other people about the Buddha.

4 I lead ceremonies and worship.

5 I visit the monastery and give food to monks.

6 I learn about the Buddha from monks.

7 The monks help me run important ceremonies.

8 I am different from everybody else, but we are all equal.

Introducing the story

This is a story of two friends who have different talents. The story is about how people are dependent on each other. It will help children to have a better understanding of the Buddhist teachings about dependence. See the notes on poster 5, the festival of Kathina Day, for more information about the relationship between monks and lay people.

Talking about the story

Teachers will use their professional judgment to ensure that this subject is treated sensitively – some/all of the children in the class will have experienced loneliness and feelings of exclusion. Ask the children

- Why was Sarah upset?
- Do you think Rebecca meant to hurt her friend?
- Can you remember being in a situation like this?
- What would you do if you knew someone who felt left out?
- What would you do if you were left out?
- How do you think Sarah and Rebecca help each other out now?

Ask the children to reflect on these questions, without necessarily replying:

- Can you think of something you are not good at?
- Who would be able to help you?
- What are you good at?
- How could you use what you are good at to help someone?

Give pairs/groups of children a piece of paper with three columns.

In the first column they should write the names or jobs of three people whom they rely on in their everyday life.

In the second column they should write what that person does for them and the community.

In the final column they should write about what it would be like if that person didn't exist.

The story of Sarah and Rebecca

Sarah and Rebecca had been best friends for as long as they could remember. They sat together in the classroom, messed around together in the playground, and went to each other's houses after school. In some ways they were quite different – Rebecca was good at maths whilst Sarah preferred sports – but when it came to chatting or sharing a story, or a game, they both liked exactly the same things.

Then one day they had a new teacher who decided to move everyone to different desks. Where they were put depended on how good they were at maths. Rebecca, who found maths really easy, was near the back. But Sarah always had to struggle to get even the simplest problems right, so she was put at the front.

Rebecca didn't mind at all: she felt good being at the top of the class, and she soon made friends with the other people she was sitting with. But Sarah was really upset. She hated not being good at maths and she couldn't understand how Rebecca could abandon her for a load of new friends, as if she wasn't good enough any more.

The weeks went by. Sarah got in with a new crowd who were really keen on running and ball games, like she was. Rebecca carried on hanging about with her new friends. It was as if the two of them had never been friends at all.

One day, in a games lesson, Sam and Emma were picking teams. Rebecca hovered at the side of the hall, feeling miserable. Everyone knew that she was dreadfully slow and clumsy; no-one ever wanted to pick her.

Sarah, on the other hand, was the first person that Sam chose for his team. One by one the others were chosen, until only Rebecca was left. Sam had to take her, but he didn't look very pleased about it.

For the first time, Rebecca suddenly realised how awful Sarah must feel when she kept getting her maths wrong.

They began to play. It was a relay race with a ball, and Sam's team soon took the lead – until it was Rebecca's turn. She felt sick with nerves as the boy in front threw his ball to her. Her fingers began to shake uncontrollably. The ball dropped from her grasp, bounced on the ground and rolled straight past her.

Everyone in the team let out a deep groan.

Because of her clumsiness, Rebecca's team lost. Rebecca's cheeks burned. She didn't dare to look at anyone.

Back in the classroom, they all started to tease her:
"Butterfingers!"
"Slow coach!"

But suddenly Sarah burst in and started to yell at them: "Shut up you lot! Rebecca can't help not being good at sport. And anyway, she's really good at maths and lots of things – much better than you! She doesn't have to be good at everything! Just leave her alone!"

Rebecca looked up in surprise. A big lump rose in her throat, but she gulped it back. "Thanks Sarah," she whispered. "I really appreciate that. I . . . I wish we could be friends again." "So do I," Sarah grinned. They smiled at each other, a little shyly.
"I tell you what," said Rebecca, "would you like me to show you how to do tonight's maths homework? After all, I think I owe you a big favour!

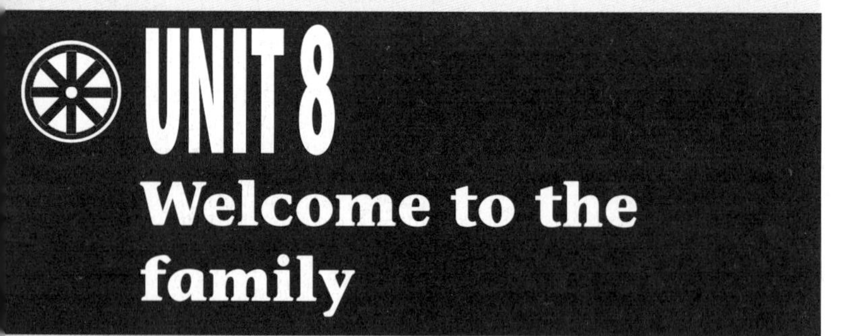

AIMS

1 The children should be able to recognise that in many/all societies babies are conventionally welcomed with presents and ceremonies.

2 The children should have conducted research into traditions in their own area.

3 The children should know about Buddhist traditions and ceremonies which welcome new babies.

PREPARATION

For these activities you will need:

- poster 8;
- copies of Activity sheet 8 (page 43);
- some pictures of gifts from a shopping catalogue ('A more basic approach', activity 4).

If possible:

- a visitor to come and give a talk about their new baby;
- a video camera or tape recorder.

Core activities

Note: Activities 1 and 2 are based on the assumption that you can arrange for a parent of a young baby to visit your class. Alternatives are suggested in the event that this is not possible.

1 Introduction and preparation
(30 mins)

The following exercises will be done in groups.

Introduce Activity 1 by telling the children that you are going to do some work on how people prepare for and welcome a new baby, and that you intend to arrange for a visit from a parent to talk about new babies.

The children have two tasks:

1 write a letter of invitation to the visitor, telling the parent why the class wants her/him to come, and what to bring;

2 prepare the questions that they would want to ask the parent during the visit.

Ensure that some reference is made to three important areas: how people prepare for the arrival of a baby; which gifts are given; which ceremonies welcome the baby.

If a suitable visitor is not available, divide the children into smaller groups. Each group should suggest questions which can be written into a class questionnaire to be taken home by children. This should provide similar information.

2 The visitor
(45 mins)

Ensure that you have prepared the visitor well for the visit, and that the children know what to ask.

The children will need to have some way of recording the responses of the parent. They are looking for information about: preparation for the baby; gifts; welcoming ceremonies and events.

Records of the visitor's answers can be made on paper. Video or tape recordings are an alternative.

The information given should be analysed and placed into three categories: preparation; gifts; welcoming ceremonies and events.

If there is no visitor, the class should analyse the information gained through the questionnaire to make lists under the three categories.

3 Looking at the poster
(15 mins)

Show the poster and use the questions and guidance on the reverse as the basis of a class discussion.

Ensure that children:

1 learn about how Buddhists prepare for, and welcome, new babies;

2 recognise similarities and differences between Buddhist customs and local customs.

4 Welcome to the family
(15 mins)

Use Activity sheet 8 (page 43) to highlight the different kinds of gift which might be expected. Look particularly for differences in gender, and gifts which are needed at different times of life.

Identify and discuss any gender stereotyping which arises, and children's reaction to this.

Stress that different religions and groups of people will have differing views about gender, and all of them should be listened to, even if they are not agreed with.

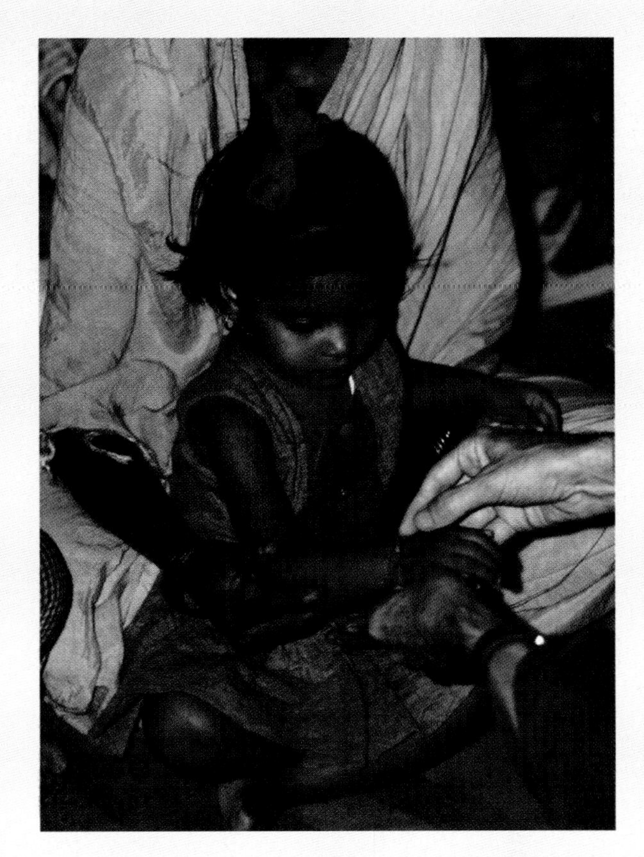

Welcome

EXTENSION

Poster 8 includes a list of the 'five precepts' which guide a Buddhist to live in a correct way. One of them is:

Do not harm living things.

Tell the children about this rule. Explain that this is not a commandment but a recommendation which is undertaken voluntarily. Bearing it in mind, they should prepare two lists of:

1 presents suitable for Buddhist babies (e.g. cotton rather than leather-made toys/clothes);

2 presents not suitable for Buddhist babies (e.g. a toy gun; an Action Man; action videos etc.).

A more basic approach

The suggestions on this page will help you adapt the Core teaching and learning activities, making them suitable for younger pupils or those at an earlier stage of development.

1 Introduction and preparation

The children will have good questions and ideas about the letter. They will need help to turn the ideas and questions into written form.

You can write a letter on behalf of the children, or write questions on cards, for use in Activity 2. Some children could copy the letter.

2 The visitor

All the children should be encouraged to ask questions. Ensure that the questions are fairly and evenly divided. Use the cards from Activity 1.

If possible, use a video/tape recorder to record the information.

Later the teacher can go through the information with the children, getting them to identify the information for the categories: preparation for the baby's arrival; gifts; welcoming ceremonies and events.

The teacher can write the words under the correct heading.

3 Looking at the poster

The questions and guidance on the reverse of the poster are suitable for all children.

You will need to record the information to go in each category.

Simple lists of words are needed so that the children can cope with Activity 4.

4 Welcome to the family

Many children will be able to copy the simple words from the lists collected in the previous activity under the heading 'gifts'.

Alternatively, find 15/20 pictures of gifts (a shopping catalogue is a good source). Include some which children have come across as Buddhist gifts (e.g. toolkit; sewing kit). Include others which have been recognised as being common from their research (e.g. fluffy toys).

Ask the children to divide the presents into two groups, and stick them into the correct column on the activity sheet.

ACTIVITY SHEET 8

Welcome to the family

Gifts given to a baby in a Buddhist family	Gifts that we know are given to babies
1 Draw . . .	1 Draw . . .
2 Draw . . .	2 Draw . . .
3 Draw . . .	3 Draw . . .

Ordination

AIMS

1. The children should understand better the meaning of an initiation or joining ceremony.
2. The children should know that ordination is an initiation ceremony for Buddhists.
3. The children should have encountered information about the ordination ceremony.
4. The children should have been able to analyse ceremonies using these categories:

   special words; special clothes; special objects or artefacts; special actions.

PREPARATION

For this unit you will need:

- a copy of *William the Intruder* by Richmal Crompton (or a suitable alternative – see Activity 1);
- poster 9;
- copies of Activity sheet 9 (page 47) and supplementary activity sheet (page 55);
- a brief version of the initiation ceremony in the story;
- a copy of the relevant parts of the information on the reverse of the poster;
- dressing-up clothes (Extension).

Core activities

1 Joining ceremonies
(30 mins)

Read the part of Chapter 2 of *William the Intruder* which describes the initiation ceremony of a squaw. (Use an alternative description of an initiation from a children's book if you would prefer.)

Introduce the children to the term 'initiation ceremony', and make sure that they understand that it is a special event when a person joins a group or organisation.

Talk with the children about the ceremony in the book, as well as their own experiences of joining ceremonies, e.g. joining Brownies, Cubs.

Identify things that such ceremonies have in common:

special words (promises or rules);

special clothes (uniforms);

special objects or artefacts;

special actions.

2 Looking at the poster
(30 mins)

Use the questions and guidance on the reverse of the poster for this activity.

3 Using the Activity sheet
(30 mins)

The activity sheet should be completed by the children.

As well as the activity sheet they will need:

1 a brief version of the initiation ceremony in the story read in Activity 1;

2 a copy of the relevant parts of the information on the reverse of the poster.

The layout of the Activity sheet will allow children to compare the ceremonies.

4 Designing an initiation ceremony
(30 mins)

Use the supplementary activity sheet (page 55).

Set the task:

- you have found out about two initiation ceremonies. Now you are going to invent your own.

Put the children into groups. Groups should be based on an interest/activity in common, e.g. football, so that they can match the symbols of that interest to the ceremony that they design.

The children can either choose the group that they join, or the teacher can allocate them to a group (perhaps in confidence, so that the other children can guess which group is being joined).

In each space on the activity sheet, the children should draw a sketch of the stages in their ceremony.

The box at the foot of each space is for a description of the activity and any special words or actions.

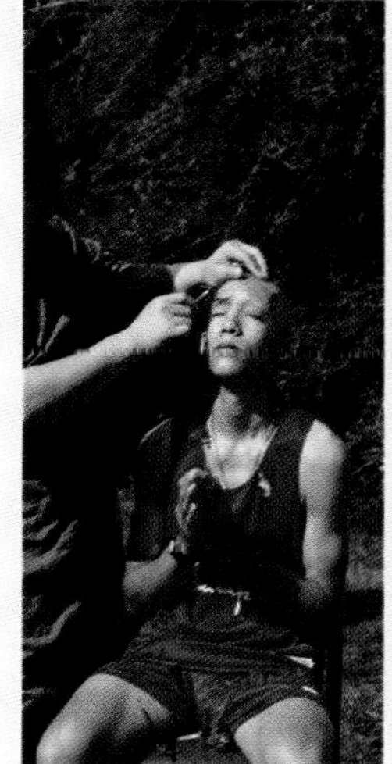

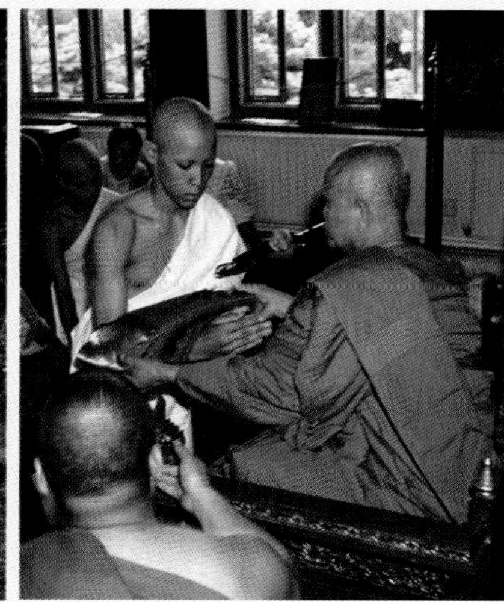

A Buddhist ordination

EXTENSION

Through Activity 4 the children have a description of an initiation ceremony and a storyboard, which can be dramatised.

Encourage the children to find suitable artefacts for use in their ceremony. Special clothing can also feature in the demonstration. Completed ceremonies can be demonstrated to the class.

Ask one child who is confident to do so, to act as a commentator on the ceremony, as if it were being broadcast. The commentary should describe the ceremony in terms of: special words; special clothes; special objects or artefacts; special actions.

A more basic approach

The suggestions on this page will help you adapt the Core teaching and learning activities, making them suitable for younger pupils or those at an earlier stage of development.

1 Joining ceremonies

The reading from *William the Intruder*, or your alternative, is appropriate for all abilities.

The term 'initiation ceremony' may be too difficult for the children. Use the phrase 'joining ceremony' instead.

Help the children recognise the things that such ceremonies have in common by: demonstrating actions; repeating words; showing examples of special clothes; having special objects available.

Encourage the children to touch the clothes and objects, to copy the actions, and repeat the special words.

2 Looking at the poster

The poster is appropriate for all abilities and ages. When talking about how the boy, the monks and the parents feel during the ceremony, write some words on flash cards and invite the children to choose which words would match each person. The words could be: frightened; proud; important; special; chosen; protective; welcoming; sad to lose their child; proud of their child.

Some words could apply to more than one character.

Prepare simple faces to denote the characters, and label them. Write the words into thought bubbles.

3 Using the Activity sheet

All children can tackle the activity sheet with assistance.

Talk with the children about the words they want to put in each box. Either write them for the children, or offer them cards with words already written on them; which they can copy or stick in the correct place. The children can draw only, where appropriate.

4 Designing an initiation ceremony

The supplementary activity sheet (page 55) can be adapted for use with all the children. Alternatively, set the task that the children are to show a scene from an initiation ceremony, as a tableau or freeze-frame.

The children can then talk about the scene that they present.

Through careful prompting, extend the scene backwards and forwards to help the children show what happens before and after the original snapshot scene.

ACTIVITY SHEET 9 **Initiation ceremonies**

	In the Buddhist ordination	In the story
Special words		
Special clothes	Draw . . .	Draw . . .
Special objects	Draw . . .	Draw . . .
Special actions	Draw . . .	Draw . . .

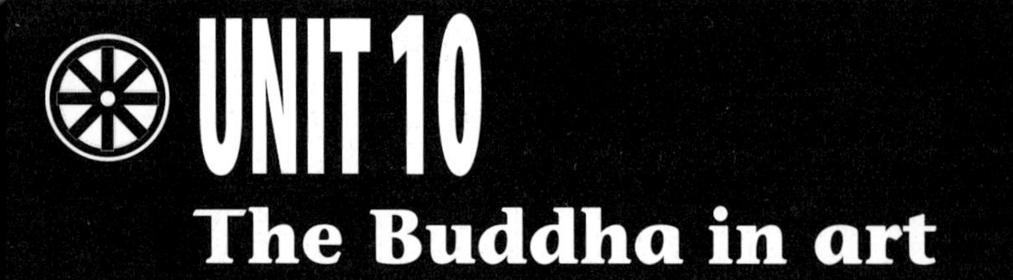

UNIT 10
The Buddha in art

AIMS

1. The children should be able to recognise that actions, gestures and facial expressions can have traditional and symbolic meaning.
2. The children should be able to recognise the symbolism in images of the Buddha.
3. The children should be familiar with the hand positions on images of the Buddha.

PREPARATION

For this unit you will need:

- poster 10;
- mime cards (Activity 1);
- copies of Activity sheet 10 (page 51) and supplementary activity sheet (page 56).

If possible:

- other pictures and a statue of the Buddha.

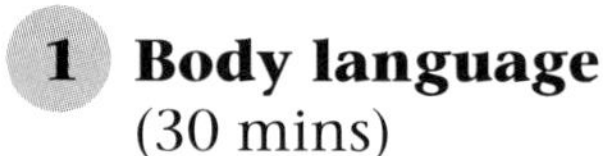

Core activities

1 Body language
(30 mins)

This activity is to extend children's understanding of how body positions and facial expressions can have commonly understood meanings. This will help them to understand that images of the Buddha have meaning.

Ask a few children to mime some simple tasks, e.g. cleaning a car; painting a door; pouring a drink.

Ask different children to mime the same activity, but give them a different character or emotion to show, e.g. happy, calm, angry, sad, thoughtful, hasty.

The activity and emotion words can be prepared on cards. Each mime can be 'frozen' whilst the rest of the children guess what the activity and emotion are supposed to be.

2 Let your fingers do the talking
(30 mins)

Use Activity sheet 10 (page 51).

This activity helps children to understand more about the symbolic and traditional meanings of hand positions and gestures, enabling them to have a better understanding of Buddhist images.

Give the children the Activity sheet. It shows ten hand positions, and gives ten sets of words which can match the positions. Children should place the words against the pictures. Some of the gestures are ambiguous and there may be more than one 'right' answer.

Ask the children to identify and demonstrate any other common (and appropriate) hand positions.

3 Looking at the poster
(30 mins)

Use the questions and guidance on the reverse of the poster as the basis of a class discussion.

Try to ensure that the children can make the link between the previous activity on body language and this activity.

4 The hands of the Buddha
(30 mins)

You will need copies of the supplementary activity sheet (page 56) for this activity. It shows some of the traditional and symbolic hand positions used in images of the Buddha.

Give out the supplementary activity sheet and look again at the poster. Ask the children:

- 'which of the hand positions on your sheet do you think is being shown on the poster?'
  (bottom left)

Talk about each of the hand positions, and their meanings.

Refer the children to what they learned in Activity 2, to link the pictures to children's experience.

Divide the class into groups. Ask each child to complete one of the hand positions on the sheet. Make sure that each of the hand positions is drawn by somebody, so that you can display the completed pictures together.

Label and display the completed pictures.

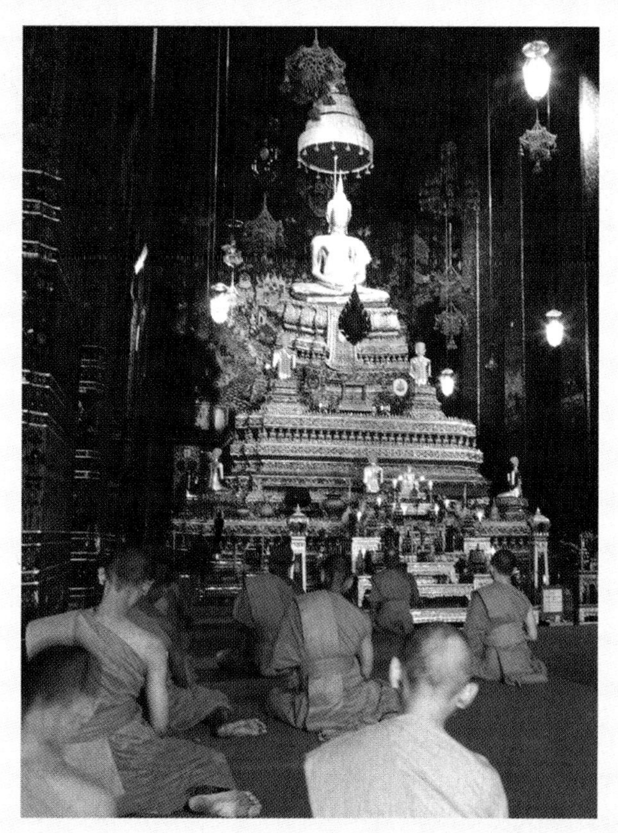

The Buddha

EXTENSION

Find other examples of images of the Buddha in textbooks. If possible, find a small statue of the Buddha.

Use additional copies of the supplementary activity sheet, or other outline drawings of the image.

Children should copy and label the drawings to show different hand positions, and their meanings.

Add these pictures to the display.

A more basic approach

The suggestions on this page will help you adapt the Core teaching and learning activities, making them suitable for younger pupils or those at an earlier stage of development.

1 Body language

This activity is suitable for all ages and abilities, although the instructions should be simplified/leading questions given, e.g.

'Show me how you would clean a car. . .';

'Show me that you are not enjoying it'.

Alternatively, ask the children to show facial expressions without relating them to one of the tasks. They use the list of words given: happy, calm, angry, sad, thoughtful, frightened.

Again, the words can be written on flash cards.

2 Let your fingers do the talking

If the children cannot cope with Activity sheet 10 (page 51), the following strategies can be used to simplify the learning:

demonstrate the gesture;

ask the children to say what you are trying to tell them with your hands and facial expression;

prepare a list of the descriptive words on cards, so that the children can choose the correct word.

Some of the children may be able to complete the activity sheet with this guidance.

3 Looking at the poster

Show the children the poster, and ask them to point out features on the picture. Explain about important features in a simple way. Do not go into detail. Ensure that they have been shown: traditional clothing; body position; hand position; flame above the head.

You can spend more time talking about their feelings and responses to the picture. Remind the children of what they did in Activity 1, and encourage them to draw links between these experiences and the expressions and body language of the Buddha. Encourage the children to find words to describe how looking at the image makes them feel.

4 The hands of the Buddha

This activity may be too demanding for some of the children. If so, you can show the line drawings of the hand positions, and picture of the Buddha on page 56.

Encourage the children to relate the hands on page 51 to the positions on the supplementary activity sheet on page 56.

ACTIVITY SHEET 10 Let your fingers do the talking

Join the words to the right hands. Talk about your answers; they may not be the same.

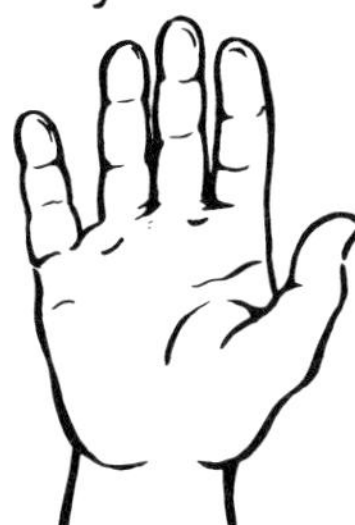
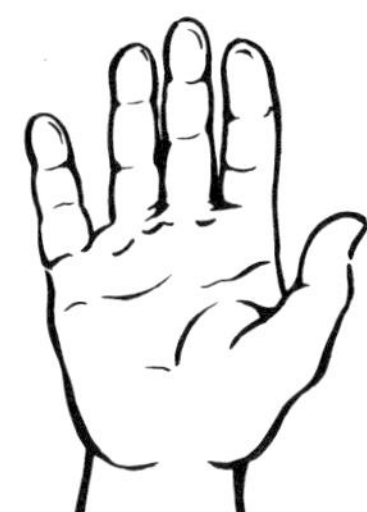

welcome please give me victory keep away

hello question prayer threat well done

UNIT 2 SUPPLEMENTARY ACTIVITY SHEET

How people concentrate

Draw or write.

How Buddhists concentrate	How I concentrate
1 Draw . . .	1 Draw . . .
2 Draw . . .	2 Draw . . .
3 Draw . . .	3 Draw . . .

UNIT 3 SUPPLEMENTARY ACTIVITY SHEET

A Buddhist shrine

Find the items you would see at a Buddhist shrine. Write the words below and describe what the item is used for.

f	l	o	w	e	r	s	t	c	u	p	s
i	h	f	a	i	d	p	a	u	b	c	n
m	r	f	e	j	s	e	b	s	n	i	e
e	b	e	q	v	e	c	l	h	o	f	h
s	q	r	s	e	g	i	e	i	r	e	p
u	n	i	c	q	o	a	d	o	b	w	v
s	e	n	k	w	d	l	w	n	n	p	s
t	l	g	o	a	t	b	e	s	t	i	e
n	q	s	t	m	l	o	p	k	n	o	g
f	w	e	y	e	i	o	n	w	s	e	w
a	i	s	t	s	n	k	o	r	i	f	s
i	n	c	e	n	s	e	s	t	n	p	e

Write the words. What is this for?

1 ______________________ → ______________________

2 ______________________ ______________________

3 ______________________ ______________________

4 ______________________ ______________________

5 ______________________ ______________________

6 ______________________ ______________________

7 ______________________ ______________________

UNIT 5 SUPPLEMENTARY ACTIVITY SHEET — The travel–game cards

Use the following statements to make cards.

CARD 1
You tell someone about the Buddha's teaching. Go on three squares. **Monks used to go around the countryside to tell people about the Buddha.**

CARD 2
You lose concentration when meditating. Miss a turn. **Meditation is an important part of Buddhist life. Buddhists believe it is one of the ways for discovering the truths about life.**

CARD 3
You are chosen to receive a new robe. Go forward two spaces. **Material for a robe is given to a monk on Kathina Day.**

CARD 4
You are very tired from your difficult travels. Miss a turn. **Monks' travels were hard. The Kathina festival took place before they went on their journeys.**

CARD 5
You meet people who live near the monastery, and enjoy their company. Go forward four spaces. **Kathina Day is a time when monks and lay people meet. They remember that the monks need the lay people to provide for their needs, and the lay people need the monks to teach them about the Buddha's teaching.**

CARD 6
The rain starts early. Go to the monastery but stay there for two goes. **In the Indian rainy season monks go to a monastery or holy place for shelter. They stay there until their travels begin again after Kathina Day.**

CARD 7
You receive many gifts on Kathina Day. Go on two places. **Gifts are given out to monks on Kathina Day. These were originally to provide the monks with food on their travels.**

CARD 8
You tear your robe. Go back three spaces. **Monks can be recognised by their orange robes.**

CARD 9
The time you have spent in retreat has helped you to understand more about the meaning of life. Move on two spaces. **A retreat is time away from ordinary, everyday life. Monks no longer travel around, but they still have a retreat. Kathina Day marks the end of retreat.**

CARD 10
You don't understand what you have read in the scriptures. Go back four spaces. **Monks read from the scriptures to find out more about the Buddha's teaching.**

UNIT 9 SUPPLEMENTARY ACTIVITY SHEET

Design an initiation ceremony

You are now a_______________________________________.

Draw a picture of one part of the joining ceremony in each box. Show six scenes from your ceremony.

In the space underneath each box, write about what is happening. Write down any special words which are spoken.

1 Draw . . .	2 Draw . . .
3 Draw . . .	4 Draw . . .
5 Draw . . .	6 Draw . . .

UNIT 10 SUPPLEMENTARY ACTIVITY SHEET

The hands of the Buddha

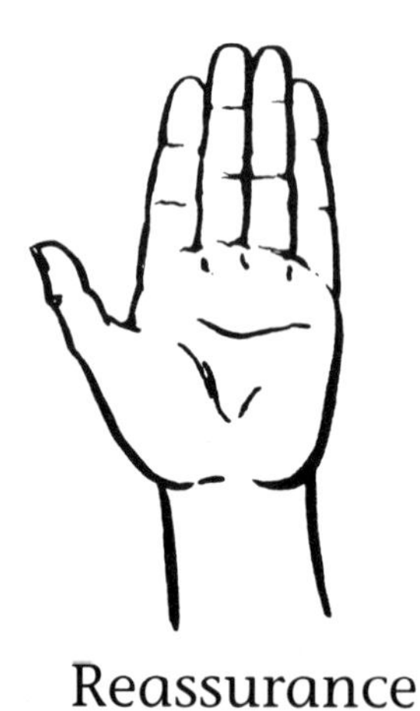

Reassurance

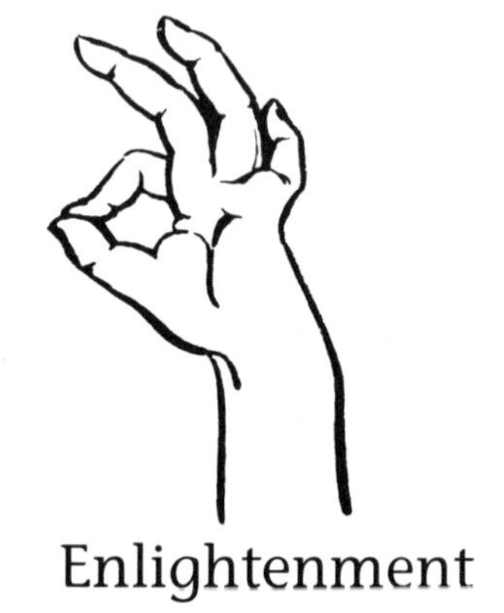

Enlightenment

Meditation

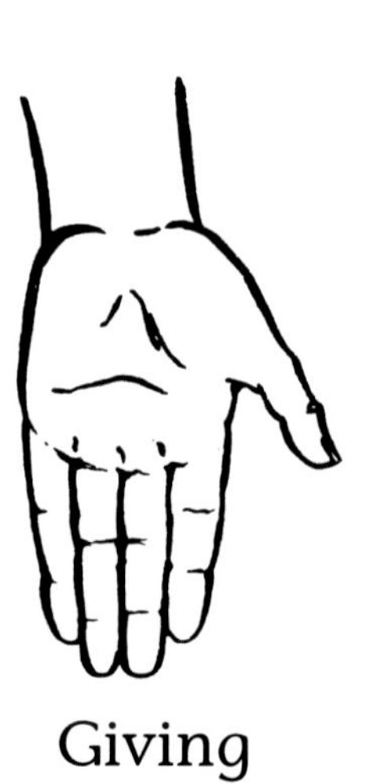

Giving

Preaching